Seeing Through The Wall

Using V.A.L.U.E. to Resolve Business and Personal Conflict

Dr. James W. Gibson

HighPoint
Publishing, Inc

Seeing Through the Wall. Text and Illustrations Copyright © 2010 by Dr. James W. Gibson. Cover Copyright © 2010 by HighPoint Publishing, Inc. All rights reserved. No part of this book may be reproduced or transmitted in any form or by any means, electronic or mechanical, including photocopying, recording or by information storage and retrieval systems – except by a reviewer, who may quote brief passages in a review to be printed in a magazine, newspaper or on the Web – without permission in writing from the publisher.

Printed and bound in the United Stated of America.

First edition. First printing 2009.

Published and distributed by:
    HighPoint Publishing, Inc.
    3975 Highway 290 East
    Dripping Springs, Texas 78620
    (512) 858–2727

Although the author and the publisher have made every effort to ensure the accuracy and completeness of information contained in this book, we assume no responsibility for errors, inaccuracies, omissions, or any inconsistency herein. Any slights of people, places or organizations are unintentional.

This book is available at quantity discounts for bulk purchases. For information, please call (512) 858–2727 or you can visit our web site at http://www.HighPointPublishing.com.

Library of Congress Control Number: 2009909836

International Standard Book Number:
    ISBN–10 1–933190–20–5
    ISBN–13 978–1–933190–20–4

Editor: Milena Christopher
Design by: Ken W. Christopher, Jr.
Production by: Ken W. Christopher, Jr.

REVIEWS AND COMMENTS

Dr. Gibson's V.A.L.U.E. System for resolving business and personal conflict is simple to initiate, easy to adapt, and achieves successful results. This book is rich with insights, tools, and guidelines.

Dr. Gibson's book should be read by all that want to manage and resolve business and everyday conflicts. The features and benefits include:

☆ a method that identifies the source, type, and extent of conflict
☆ step by step guidelines for implementation
☆ ready to use tools and techniques
☆ scenarios for illustration
☆ lays the foundation for future positive interactions

Sandy Leasure
Investor, and former owner of the first McDonald's franchise in Texas ... Huntsville, Texas

REVIEWS AND COMMENTS

I find the content imperative and the approach interest–catching and effective. Even after a short while of practicing the V.A.L.U.E. System, I'm convinced the techniques work.

Ellen B. Brown
Attorney at Law

ACKNOWLEDGMENTS

First, I need to thank my many former students, business associates, and family for encouraging me to write this book. I finally got tired of hearing "you need to put this system in a book so more people can learn the process."

Of course, a huge debt of gratitude goes to my editors Ken and Milena Christopher for their creative talent in the book design… including the title, and the idea of a "Wall Series" of future conflict resolution books. Look for them.

Without critical review, this book would not have had the character it deserves. Therefore, I need to thank a former co-author and friend, Kirk Blackard, not only for his critical review but also for his suggestions on clarity and readability. Also, Mary Martha Stinnett, Janice Gipson, Karen London and Sandy Leasure made insightful content and graphic suggestions that were used throughout the book.

Also, I want to express my appreciation to all those that have allowed me to use their names and "stories" as examples within these pages. The other names and "stories"... who knows where they came from. Maybe some of my readers will recognize themselves within these pages. If so, thank you also.

Lastly, thank you Lord for keeping me alive these last few years to complete and publish this book. May people be blessed through reading this book and your grace!

FOREWORD

Standing atop one section of the Great Wall of China, I see this massive wall snake for miles in front and back of me. There appears to be no end to this great structure of ancient times. Only low lying clouds can obstruct its presence. The Great Wall of China also reminds me of continuing conflict and other famous walls of conflict such as the Berlin Wall in Germany.

On a business and personal level there are walls just as great and just as powerful. Walls that separate, hold back, block, restrain, and prevent communication that would resolve conflict. Many walls are psychologically defensive walls, and many are built from fear of either conflict engagement or the past results of conflict. Whatever form each wall takes the result is an impediment to engaging or resolving conflict.

"Seeing through the Wall" describes a method, through a unique approach called the V.A.L.U.E. System, that will enable you to see through the "walls" of conflict that occur daily in your business and person life. Knowing that the V.A.L.U.E. System works and how to use the V.A.L.U.E. System to engage and manage everyday conflict provides you the courage to see your way through any wall of conflict and begin to engage your conflicts at the earliest possible stage.

Knowing how to see your way through conflict is a profound key to conflict management. The V.A.L.U.E. System, properly applied, leads to greater productivity in business and greater personal satisfaction in relationships. Because conflict in our lives is real and enduring, just like the Great Wall of China, it is essential that you obtain this key. Not only must you obtain the key, but also use it for seeing through your walls of conflict.

The chapters that follow allow you to possess V.A.L.U.E. … the knowledge to see your way through each conflict wall you encounter. Possessing V.A.L.U.E., and gaining the skills necessary to apply V.A.L.U.E., will empower you to engage and manage conflict without fear of loss, giving in, being put down or depreciated as a person. So grab the V.A.L.U.E. key and begin a new adventure of seeing through your conflict walls.

P-167

Validation (does not equal agreement)

Add your perspective

Learn (how to learn)

U (understand the differences and distinctions

Empower — how to empower

Seeing Through
The Wall

TABLE OF CONTENTS

Preface

Chapter One
PEOPLE FEAR CONFLICT 5
   The Real World 5
   Coping With Conflict 9
   Assuming Personal Responsibility For
   Managing Conflict 11
   What To Expect 16

Chapter Two
THE TROUBLE WITH CONFLICT 21
   Defining Conflict. 21
   The Pathology of Conflict 23
   Popular Ways To Avoid Engaging
   Personal Conflict. 28
   Conflict Alienates People. 35
   Conflicts Positive Side 37
   Engaging Conflict. 39
   How To Manage Conflict Effectively . . . 43

Chapter Three
THE V.A.L.U.E. SYSTEM 45
   Benefits of the V.A.L.U.E. System 45
   Recycle Personal Conflicts. 46
   Enhance Relationships 47
   No Fight or Flight Attitude 48
   Maintain Control of Conflict 48
   Manage and Move On. 49

New Skills for Old Problems 50
Recognize Conflict Earlier 50
The V.A.L.U.E. Process. 52
How the V.A.L.U.E. Process Works 54
Communications Issues 61
Let's Get Started 63

Chapter Four
V.A.L.U.E. BLOCK ONE: VALIDATION . . 67
What is Validation? 67
Validate Early and Often. 75
Steps to Validation. 80
Utilize Listening Skills. 84
The Timing of Validation 85
Improper Validation 86
Validation Sets the Agenda 87

Chapter Five
V.A.L.U.E. BLOCK TWO: ADD YOUR PERSPECTIVE. 91
Add Your Perspective 91
Organize Your Perspective/Position . . . 95
Keep Issues to Three. 97
Use Simple Words and Phrases 98
Your Beliefs Can Be Different 99
Be Non–Threatening and Factual 100
Use "I" Based Statements 101
Use "Need" Based Statements 102
Hidden Agendas 103
The Effect of Adding Your
Perspective, Idea or Belief 104

Chapter Six
V.A.L.U.E. BLOCK THREE: HOW TO LEARN............................107
    Learn 107
    Power Imbalances................. 108
    Transforming and Recycling Issues... 112
    Transform New Knowledge Into Concepts 113

Chapter Seven
V.A.L.U.E. BLOCK FOUR: HOW TO UNDERSTAND THE DIFFERENCES AND DISTINCTIONS....................135
    Understand Distinctions and Differences 135
    Distinctions and Differences 136
    Exploring the Sub–Parts............ 139
    Look for the Same Sub–Parts 141
    Contrast the Sub–Parts 141
    Inquire About the Difference 142
    Stress Needs, Values, Beliefs and Perceptions 144
    Try to Make an Equation of Meaning.. 145
    Dealing with Hidden Agendas or Resistance 152
    An Observation on the Process 153

Chapter Eight
V.A.L.U.E. BLOCK FIVE: HOW TO EMPOWER 157
    Empower Resolution............... 157

How to Empower Resolution 158
The Empowerment Plan 162
An Empowerment Plan Outline 163
Non-Resolution 166
Re-Visiting the Conflict at a Later
Time – "Truce". 166
Walking Away with Dignity
and Self-Worth 167

Chapter Nine
THE V.A.L.U.E. GUIDE. 169

Chapter Ten
ILLUSTRATIONS OF THE V.A.L.U.E.
SYSTEM. 177
The V.A.L.U.E. System in Personal
Interactions 177
The V.A.L.U.E. System in Consumer
Affairs. 181
The V.A.L.U.E. System in Family
Disputes. 186
The V.A.L.U.E. System in Landlord/Tenant
Disputes. 197

KEY POINTS 203
Chapter 1. 203
Chapter 2. 204
Chapter 3. 204
Chapter 4. 205
Chapter 5. 206

Table of Contents

Chapter 6. 207
Chapter 7. 208
Chapter 8. 208

LIST OF DIAGRAMS 209

ABOUT THE AUTHOR 213

To the three brightest stars in my firmament ...

Betty,

Kathryn,

and Allyson

Begin challenging your own assumptions. Your assumptions are your windows on the world. Scrub them off every once in awhile, or the light won't come in.
Alan Alda

Preface

Seeing Through The Wall

"And, I don't do windows!" What a funny statement. It sounds like a line drawn in the sand or a declaration of independence. These are my thoughts as a child remembering the responses my mother received while interviewing for help around our home. This response worries me. I can't figure it out in my mind. Why don't people clean windows? Finally I ask my mother. She quickly responds, "It's simply too much to expect these days." These days refers to the 1960's. Today it's ,"I don't do conflict!" What a funny statement. I can't reconcile that declaration in my mind until I remember what my mother said, "That's simply too much to expect these days."

These days are the twenty–first century, and these times are overwhelmed with personal, domestic, and international conflict. It's not so much the conflict, it's the cleaning up of conflict that people don't do. Conflict is just like a window. Unless you clean the window, it gets dirtier and dirtier until your view becomes distorted.

Why don't people clean their conflict windows more often? Why let conflict dirty up our view of life? Because most people don't possess conflict management skills, therefore, as my mother said, "It's simply too much to expect these days." Also, the fear of conflict's negative consequences is too great based upon most people's past experiences. Although I was a strapping young boy, I never played football. I didn't want to get hurt. My thinking was logical for a boy of five who passed out when knocked down by a fast and hard football. I'm five, but I'm not dumb. Not to be daunted, my dad takes me hunting. I freeze in the cold and rain. And, I don't do hunting!

Fear of the consequences of conflict is real. However, most of us don't have a good track record in conquering this fear. The reason is simple. We were never taught how to properly engage and manage conflict. Our parents didn't teach us nor did our schools. My church told me to follow the "Golden Rule" of do unto others as you would have them do to you. That rule was not so "golden" for me on the school yard in grade school.

Most people in the world today have no proper training in conflict resolution, and certainly no personal system for

Preface

engaging and managing conflict. Therefore when people are forced into conflict the personal consequences are disastrous. The goal of this book is to provide you with a simple five block system (the V.A.L.U.E. System) to engage, manage, and gain positive results from conflict. Conquering conflict means learning to properly engage conflict by learning conflict resolution techniques and working a simple system ... the V.A.L.U.E. System.

This book will aid you in resolving conflict in everyday life. Once you become comfortable with using the five easy blocks, conflict issues that develop in relationships will become clearer and easier to manage. Thus, your normal relationships with others will improve. Not only will this book educate you on how to properly engage and manage conflict, but also it will teach you the five building blocks for conflict resolution. The building blocks of the V.A.L.U.E. system (Validate, Add, Learn, Understand, and Empower) are not difficult to learn. In fact, many reading this book will recognize some of these building blocks. Many readers may already be using one or two in conversations with others. However, this book combines these blocks in a different way for success in conflict resolution management.

Each chapter will explain the reason behind a building block. You will know why you are using that building block. You will also be given a full explanation of how to use each building block. Many examples and visual diagrams will aid you in quickly grasping the techniques of each building block. You will even be given the exact words to use for each block of the process. Later you can adapt these words to your own communication style to make the V.A.L.U.E. System part of your everyday conversations when needed. At the end of the book is a concise guide containing the basic information of each block of the V.A.L.U.E. System. The guide organizes the information as to when to use it, how to use it, and what to say.

Like anything new, it may take a little practice to obtain maximum effectiveness. Therefore, follow this plan for success:

- ❖ First, read the book from cover to cover. Don't skip any section, and don't worry about learning it all at one time.
- ❖ Second, go back to the first building block, VALIDATION, and read that chapter. Validate people for one week, referring back to the chapter as needed during the week.
- ❖ Next, follow this same procedure for the ADD, LEARN, UNDERSTAND, and EMPOWER chapters.

After a few short weeks of reading and practice you will be on the road to a new V.A.L.U.E. in your life. Good reading, good practice, and good conflict management.

Chapter One

If we cannot now end our differences, at least we can make the world safe for diversity.
John F. Kennedy

PEOPLE FEAR CONFLICT

The Real World

Feeling the cold point of a gun at his head, Cecil fears death as he attempts to shield his son's body from a masked robber's bullet. Lying on top of his son, Cecil thinks to himself ... "Maybe the bullet will lodge in my body and then Wade will live to see another day." "I love you son," he whispers. The robber shouts, "Follow instructions and nobody gets hurt! Lady give me your jewelry, now! Okay, lady, face down on the floor. No one move for thirty minutes. Hear me?" Cecil, Wade and Lynda freeze on the den floor and listen as the masked robber slams the back door. After a few deadly quiet moments they whisper to each other, "Is it over? How did this happen in our neighborhood, and to us? What is wrong with people today?"

On April 20, 1999, television pictures of a high school massacre shock millions of viewers. How many students were killed? Who did this? Why? Drawing into ourselves we search for answers to this human reality check. Our eyes fixate on television coverage with shocking pictures of hysterical students escaping death. Our ears burn as the horrible, shocking reports rebound on our senses. There has been a student massacre at Columbine High School in seemingly peaceful Littleton, Colorado. Conflict and hatred explode as horror becomes sadness, and sadness prompts both unanswered questions and fear for the future. How could these Columbine High School students in peaceful Littleton, Colorado perform such hideous crimes? Why were these students and teachers killed? What is wrong with our youth? What is wrong with our world?

Fast forward to September 11, 2001. I am walking across campus to my office and laughing out loud at a student's conversation on her cell phone. Loudly she questions, "A plane hit the World Trade tower in New York City?" I thought, "What a ridiculous joke. The caller really knows how to get her attention". However in my office, stillness prompts a sense of apprehension. My student assistant's attention is fixed on his computer monitor. As I glance at his monitor a plane crashes into a New York City landmark. Time appears to slow as tragic scenes repeat in visual horror. A New York City skyscraper crumbles to ash and debris. People flee, soot covers everyone making them appear like ghosts, panic and pain abound. The order of normal life disappears as the harsh reality of terror sinks into peoples' minds. The death tolls rise as this horrible day unfolds.

Conflict repeats itself in London on July 7, 2005 as three different tube passenger cars explode and one double-decker bus blows up less than one hour later. The coordinated attack kills 56 people. Fortunately, a terrorist plot is discovered and spoiled in August of 2006 preventing the explosion of a United States passenger plane about to leave London, England for the United States of America. International conflict escalates to the point of being uncontrolled by the existing systems of governments established to protect people through civil order.

On Monday, April, 16, 2007 a student opens fire in a dorm and classroom at a university in Virginia, Virginia Tech, killing at least 30 people in the deadliest shooting rampage in U. S. history. The shooting spreads panic and confusion on campus, with witnesses reporting students jumping out the windows of a classroom building to escape the gunfire. SWAT teams with helmets, flak jackets and assault rifles swarm over the campus. Students and faculty members carry out some of the wounded themselves, without waiting for ambulances to arrive. Finally the gunman is killed, bringing the death toll to 31.

On Valentine's day February 14, 2008, Steven Kazmierazak opens fire on students in a geology class at Northern Illinois University in DeKalb, Illinois. This former student in the master's program at the University's School of Social Work not only injures eighteen students but also kills five scholars and himself. Anandhi Narasimhan, a Los

Seeing Through The Wall

Angeles psychiatrist is quoted in February 18th, 2008 <u>U. S. A. Today</u> as saying, "People all of a sudden don't wake up one day and become violent in this nature. Usually there was something going on."

With international terrorism, small–town mass killings, robbery and personal death threats, conflict at the highest level instills fear of the future and loss of control over our lives. A conflicted, rapidly changing world creates a malaise over our future, not to mention the result of stress from living daily with conflicts. Conflicts abound with war, work, family, religion, loss of retirement earnings when the stock market fluctuates, and the world economy. People's lists go on and on. Personal stress builds which in turn fosters more conflict. Psychologists counsel depressed people with sad situational events. From the welfare system to the peer pressure of schools, individuals are involved in systems that create conflict. Like an old–fashioned pressure cooker or steam boiler, when the pressure gets too high and there is no adequately functioning relief valve, explosions happen. The result is a simple principle of physics ... an explosion.

Sadly, these international, United States and personal conflicts that escalate to violence are examples of episodes which demonstrate what intuitively we already know. As a world population, we are out of control not only with international conflicts, but also with our personal conflicts. You know the buildup of conflict is real because you see and feel it everyday. For example, news of a suspected terrorist chemical agent attack, a flu pandemic, or a declining financial market can depress us. Perhaps a close friend is considering divorce or you come home from a long day at work only to be confronted with a family problem. Chances are conflict plays an active role in your life and is likely building.

Coping With Conflict

The quality of our lives depends not on whether or not we have conflicts, but on how we respond to them.
Tom Crum

In order to cope, we try to control more of our environment. After the "9–11 incident" an increase in police power and national security was instigated in the United States of America. Much of the control factor involves attempting to control actions of other people or nations. Unfortunately, such control may lead to abusive or violent behavior, which is the last stop in a journey from a small disagreement to outright hostility – conflict manifest in a pathology that will be explored in Chapter II.

From a conflict resolution perspective, all of us need to recognize that our conventional power systems are breaking down because the world cannot be maintained in discrete compartments separated by walls, borders, seas, ideologies, or other barriers. Due to space travel, the internet, the world economy, satellites and technological advances, our mental and physical worlds have no borders or barriers that cannot be crossed or violated. Although governments forge alliances for their survival in this global economy, individuals still feel isolated, insecure, and seek even more personal security in order to obtain greater inner peace.

The popularity of religion today is evidence of the individual's search for security. Religions offer an escape valve for people of all nationalities. People flock to their place of worship to gain the sense of personal security and peace they desire in a conflicted world. Spirituality and the search for inner peace and security prosper today as people seek a way to bring peace to their lives. Interestingly, the tenets of spirituality and wellness teach facing of personal issues that appear to cause conflict. Accordingly, avoidance or denial of conflicts keeps a person bound to their fears. Exploring issues and attempting to work on these issues is empowering. From a conflict management perspective, the V.A.L.U.E. System opens up and explores issues in order to empower individuals.

KEY POINT

Although today the outright manifestations of conflict are spotlighted by terrorism, hate crimes and violent acts of aggression, we all must realize that our government or other institutions are not adept enough to resolve these problems. Each of us must learn to engage and manage conflict in order to solve our own problems which will, in turn, cause a collective shift in the problem re-solving capacity of our culture. No longer can we hide from this personal responsibility. Each of us has to learn how to manage and resolve conflict in our own personal world of accountability.

Chapter One

Without a new plan for personal conflict resolution, many individuals will maintain insulated and isolated lives due to unresolved conflict or lack of a better way to work with conflict in their lives. Unless something constructive is done by each of us on a very personal level to relieve the continual conflict and stress in our lives, we will find ourselves relating to each other by personal computer, and the steel bars on our homes will become bars to the full enjoyment of our lives.

ASSUMING PERSONAL RESPONSIBILITY FOR MANAGING CONFLICT

Albert Einstein said, "The reason we can't solve our current problems is that we are looking at them in the same way we did in the past." Einstein wisely means look at solving problems differently, and then we will see a different solution. Currently, asserting power is the favored way for people and nations to solve conflict issues. Assertion of power works because force does "solve" a conflict ... in the short run. On the other hand, exerting power does not allow a method to "re–solve" people's underlying needs nor a method to "re–solve" the underlying problems. However, power solutions by their nature separate individuals and nations into winners and losers. After the "9–11" attacks, the tension between the United States of America versus the terrorist nations grew. As the United States of America regrouped with international allies for protection and safety, a strong message of "us" versus "them" resounded around the world. Such messages of protective hostility escalate conflict from confrontation to war. Normally, conflicts between national ideologies tend to ferment; however, the 9–11 attacks quickly appeared to escalate the ideological conflict from mere fermentation into a war.

Unless we, as individuals or groups, learn to properly engage conflict with our adversaries, a pathology of turmoil will ensue, complete with the sudden pronouncement of hostile words or actions, which ultimately may lead to a personal "war".

KEY POINT

As Einstein implies, we must re–look at issues in a new way. In other words, we must learn a process to "re–solve" our personal conflict. We need to adopt a new personal process to properly engage and resolve conflict right from the start. An effective resolution process incorporates interpersonal action and thought. Thus, *we can look at conflict differently. We can also discover a process to foster resolution of conflict.*

The V.A.L.U.E. System utilizes a method of communication that fosters relationships that work in the long run for personal and global peace. The ultimate resolution of global conflict starts with individuals who seek personal peace, and are willing to appropriately

Chapter One

confront their own personal conflict issues. No longer can individuals rely on the present systems of delegated governmental or institutional power to control the spread of global conflict. Throughout history governmental power has never been a match for individuals with passion and those set upon reaching a goal, whether for evil or good: Joan of Arc, Adolf Hitler, Martin Luther King, Malcolm X, Nelson Mandela to name a few notables.

Delegating responsibility to solve our problems is always easier than assuming personal responsibility for conflict resolution. Thus, many people have grown up with the idea that "others" are here to resolve our problems. The courts, the legislatures, political parties, assistance programs, the police, the church, friends, relatives, or the boss will rescue us from our conflict. The list of power-enablers stretches out like a desert road seen from the top of a hill on a summer day..., beautiful, but hot to the touch.

As previously mentioned, personal and work conflicts are ever-present in our daily lives. Conflict embodies force and power. That power will either operate negatively or positively ... rarely is it neutral. It is our individual choice as to this outcome. When we begin to manage the forces of conflict properly, we transform the nature of conflict in our daily lives. We also transform the power of conflict into the power of personal character because we make a decision to engage and process conflict constructively. This vital decision changes the way other people see us, hear us, and feel our presence. Once we are guided by a workable conflict management system, we cease to be fearful of conflict, and increase our dignity and sense of character. We can now turn conflict management into an aspect of our character.

For many years my own true character suffered because I chose to avoid conflict. I would not serve on boards where I felt the company did not want to deal ethically with customers. I tried to satisfy other people's needs since I felt they were more powerful than mine. Employers loved me because I never made waves on the job, and I worked overtime to avoid criticism. In order to avoid interpersonal conflicts in the job market, I even started working for myself. I filtered out conflict so well that much of reality did not apply to me. It was always the other guy who was having financial troubles or getting a divorce. Sure, my life was not easy, but my family and I had no major problems. I saw myself as lucky but, looking back, I was foolish. I avoided conflicts by compromising what I really wanted, which included being treated well by others and having what I needed. And while I manipulated situations to evade problems, I usually manipulated myself into believing I could effectively eliminate conflict in my life. After the build up of stress eventually made me ill, I saw that my attempt to eliminate conflict affected my health and happiness. I knew I must take personal responsibility for engaging, as opposed to controlling my conflicts. Denial no longer works in my life.

Chapter One

After this time, I set out to learn as much as I could about conflict resolution theory and how to avoid the traps that had radically altered my health, relationships, and life. I read many books on how to communicate, be productive, make friends, influence others, or manipulate people in negotiation. But none spoke to a workable system of personal conflict resolution. None spoke to taking personal responsibility for conflict resolution. I then discovered my own system (the V.A.L.U.E. System) through research and practice. Teaching this system of conflict resolution surprised me with the results. Individuals finishing my courses always spoke the same mantra, "Even if I never mediate a case, I will still use the skills learned in class to control conflict in my personal and business life." And not surprisingly, students report greater happiness in their family and business lives. Therefore, thanks to my students' feedback this book is written to introduce others to the V.A.L.U.E. System, a workable, five–block process that will help individuals manage their conflicts and in turn promote a happier, healthier life.

In reality, some conflicts, problems, or personal relationships cannot be resolved in a reasonable time. But the parties can agree to work on some type of resolution that leaves each person with a position of respect without asserting blame. Also, it is important to note that the system will not fully operate in certain circumstances – some individuals may be impaired by drug use or psychological problems; such disabilities may affect results even for the most adept at using any form of conflict resolution … but the V.A.L.U.E. System can still serve as an armor to protect against the fear of the consequences of confrontation. If you have worked the V.A.L.U.E. System in such situations, you have done your best and can decide to move past the conflict.

What To Expect

Chapter II explores conflict, conflict avoidance and the need for active conflict engagement and management. Adequately defining conflict, and how conflict develops and grows, helps the reader to more fully understand the true nature of conflict in order to be comfortable in engaging problems and managing them through the V.A.L.U.E. System. Understanding that conflict, properly managed, can have positive results will reinforce the use of conflict management techniques.

Chapter III is an overview of the benefits of the V.A.L.U.E. System and how the system works. There you will see the process as one of:

- **VALIDATING** each person and his or her issues, beliefs, or values without having to agree in principle.
- **ADDING** your perspective.
- **LEARNING** the other person's perspective.
- **UNDERSTANDING** the meaning behind the other person's perspective. Others in turn understand

Chapter One

your perspective by exploring the distinctions that make–up these perspectives.

* **EMPOWERING** yourself and the other person with options that are win/win for resolution.

Chapters IV through VIII will fully explore, describe, and explain each of the above elements of the system with examples and key concepts. At the end of each chapter will be a guide on each block. The guide will give you the definition of each element, when to use the element and the exact words to use. Chapter IX will pull together the complete system in the handy complete guide. Chapter X will give specific illustrations of the V.A.L.U.E. System in consumer, employment, domestic relations and other conflicts.

As previously described, you will find helpful the guide in Chapter IX with specific words and phrases to use with the V.A.L.U.E. System. Each section from Validation to Empowerment will set out the key concepts and the proper words and phrases to use for the desired results. You can carry this guide around with you for quick reference until these words and phrases become second nature to you. As you progress with the concept of engaging conflict, you may decide to tweak some of the words and phrases to fit your personal style and personality. That decision is fine as long as you are achieving the same desired results from the system. The goal is to integrate the process into your daily habits so V.A.L.U.E. becomes a natural part of your communication. In essence, properly engaging and managing conflict will *be* part of your new nature.

This system works because it exposes the root of conflict and deals with the perceived *differences* and distinctions in perspectives that separate our thinking. In the concept of the V.A.L.U.E. System, differences mean perceptions that are opposite. Distinctions are different characteristics of the same concept ... the subparts. Most books on conflict management offer methods for compromise or ways to find common ground to settle disputes. This tactic depreciates the person or his ideas. Such a position sends a message that if I can't agree with the other person, then I will have to compromise my beliefs or values. People don't like to be compromised as individuals; therefore, such a message deters them from engaging in conflict. Thus, they try many methods to avoid conflict as we will discuss in Chapter II. This book teaches you how to effectively deal with *differences* between each individual's perceptions, which we call distinctions. Such exploration of distinctions in individual perceptions produces <u>new information</u>. It is only when one has been given new and different information that it is possible to find new options for resolution of conflict.

Whatever your present position in life, a single working mom raising children alone or a business executive dealing with conflict in your organization, the V.A.L.U.E. System, in almost every context, will work for you in your daily life. Begin to Validate people and their ideas. Then properly Add your perspective. Next

Chapter One

Learn, in depth, the specifics of your adversaries issues. Seek out and Understand the differences and perceptual distinctions in your specific meaning of issues and theirs. Dialogue, then build on these distinctions to create new information for options for resolution. Empower each other with a resolution that acknowledges new win/win options.

At first, this process may sound very complicated to you. The feeling that, "I can't do this" is normal. And I Validate that feeling. I would also like to Add that you need to give yourself a chance to see what you can accomplish after reading and working the system over a several week period. You don't have to be perfect the first time you try. Just like learning to ride a bicycle … it may take a few tries until you get the feel of the proper balance to ride the bike. Above all, don't worry about your ability to work the system … the system and the appropriate words will come to you! After several weeks, you will begin to substitute your own words and phrasings. Don't give up! Follow the weekly guide on page 3 of the Preface.

That which we persist in doing becomes easier, not that the task has become easier, but that our ability to perform it has improved.
Ralph Waldo Emerson

Chapter Two

We should be careful to get out of an experience only the wisdom that is in it – and stop there; lest we be like the cat that sits down on the hot stove–lid. She will never sit down on a hot stove–lid again, and that is well; but also she will never sit down on a cold one any more.
Mark Twain

THE TROUBLE WITH CONFLICT

Defining Conflict

Many people prefer to define conflict as particular situations set in time. Therefore, a lawsuit, war, divorce, physical violence or lack of agreement would define conflict. Such examples define situational conflict. Conflict as a concept is broader. Conflict has stages of growth that give it an ongoing life of its own. Although apparently good relationships exist between individuals or nations, fermenting conflict continues below the surface. The typical phrase, "Things are going so well there must be something wrong," expresses the perception that underlying conflict exists in the best of relationships. Also, the root of conflict is difficult to pinpoint even though the outward manifestations of an eruption of conflict appear at a particular time and place. Like a volcano, conflict bubbles and vents dangerous fumes long before an eruption of words or actions. Conflict needs constant monitoring in the same way geologists watch and take samples of volcanic materials attempting to predict eruptions. Conflict, like a volcano, can stay dormant or proceed to eruption depending upon the environmental factors.

KEY POINT

Conflict is an *ongoing* state of disagreement or disharmony that has the potential to ultimately advance from fermentation to a state of open, prolonged fighting or war.

For example, you may have a difference of opinion with your superior about how work is to be performed in your area of responsibility. Discussions with your supervisor produce no resolution; therefore, work is performed as the supervisor wants. But you feel these procedures cost the company a decline in employee morale and more money in the long run. This underlying conflict continues to ferment and remains ongoing.

Chapter Two

The Pathology of Conflict

Conflict, like cancer, has a definite pathology. Recognizing this pathology, with all its ramifications, allows an understanding not only of what behaviors escalate conflicts, but also at what stage conflict openly presents itself. Rarely does an outright hostile encounter present itself without warning if one knows what to look for beforehand. Like a volcano or a hurricane, conflict builds up or fizzles out due to various environmental factors that feed or diminish its strength. The first and underlying stage is fermentation.

Fermentation

During the fermentation stage, people perceive differences in their circumstances or incompatible interests between themselves and others. However, individuals don't act upon these differences. For example, a new supervisor has been appointed from outside the company ranks. Suddenly an awareness of new management policies begins to gnaw at company old-timers and cause them distress. At this stage, nothing is mentioned by the old school employees, but under the surface of politeness or politically correct communication, a conflict is brewing. The conflict, caused by change in management policies, will ferment as long as there is no person, group, faction, or institution that is identified as the activating cause of the distress. As long as general distress is only recognized, without placing blame or causation on a specific entity, fermentation will continue without conflict advancing into the second stage. During fermentation, people may decide they can live (for any number of personal reasons) with the differences causing the distress.

> ### KEY POINT
>
> *What often looks like no conflict is really circumstances fermenting or breaking down.* Think of developing conflict as the process of making a delicious fruit topping from scratch. My mother makes a delicious dessert topping by using a starter solution to break down and dissolve fresh fruit. But the process takes time to chemically work. Although I open the covered bowl and sense nothing happening, the starter solution is fermenting and chemically breaking down the fruit. What appears on the surface as nothing happening is not reality. The dessert process is called fermentation or a process of breaking things down. Conflict works the same way in its first stage.

But more often than not, one person looks outward to determine the cause of her distress. Perhaps you and your business associate get along well, yet suddenly tempers flare as you discuss plans on a new work assignment. The new work assignment is cutting-edge, and your business associate wants you to use old techniques … thus the cause for this difference. Maybe your significant other, after years of a seemingly romantic relationship, wants to leave you. The result of this fermenting conflict hits unexpectedly. Conflict events surprise people unless they realize that conflict is always brewing or fermenting. Looking back, there may have been signs of your business associate not valuing continuing education training or spousal unhappiness which were missed or denied.

Awareness

The next phase of conflict development is awareness that someone or something (a person, policy, or rule) has the power to either give or deprive you of what you perceive you want or need. A new supervisor is appointed. Both of you have different ideas regarding the interpretation of company policies. You now realize that your flex–time will be different than with your previous supervisor who was promoted. You are now aware that a conflict may be coming over flex–time. If not abated, conflict goes into it third phase, confrontation.

Confrontation

Confrontation develops when the awareness of deprivation of needs is acted upon. At this point, blame is connected to or placed on another entity as the culprit. This placing of blame is declared openly and for the purpose of correcting the resulting actual or perceived distress that a person, policy, or rule has the power to deprive you of what you want or need. During the confrontation stage, perceptions of evil, harm, shame, and guilt play a big part in drawing the confrontation to a head. Also during this stage, parties become polarized in their positions of right and wrong, good and bad or other extremes. As the confrontation grows, it becomes more open and obvious. The battle lines are clearly drawn at the end of this stage. The parties are simply waiting to fight it out for better or for worse … they don't care.

In our previous example of an employee with a new supervisor, the confrontation stage would arrive when the new supervisor denied the employee flex–time, in a situation in which flex–time bad been granted by her former supervisor. At this time the employee sees the new supervisor as depriving her of her rightful flex–time. She will blame the new supervisor, and file a formal complaint to evidence the confrontation. Therefore, without a proper system in place to engage the hostility of the hostile employee at this confrontation stage, conflict can escalate into violence.

Violence

If there is no workable intervention strategy at this point, one party may determine that power (in the form of violence) will be the only solution to the distress. Open aggression in the form of violence can be set off quite suddenly by an event which would normally be considered incidental. Tempers are high and minds that would normally be rational shut down. The focus is on "hurting" the other person as much as possible. We have all seen many examples of this ranging from divorce proceedings (think of the movie "The War of the Roses") to fighting in bars, not to mention union battles at picket lines as well as battles between police and protesters.

War

The last and final phase of conflict is violence on a small or large scale of death and destruction. A common example is what is now termed "going postal." In these past incidences, postal workers appear fine one day, and the next day the postal employee comes to work and shoots other postal workers or supervisors. For the individual, declared war is rare as an ultimate result of conflict. However, there are incidences of conflict that ensnare individuals in the larger web of conflict. The destruction and death at the World Trade Center on 9–11–2001 is a perfect example as well as other international wars throughout the history of mankind. Unfortunately, without a national or international system to prevent ideological conflict from escalating, wars and destruction are inevitable.

Popular Ways To Avoid Engaging Personal Conflict

Even if we know the pathology of conflict, to even consider trying to manage all the conflict in our lives is exhausting. Thus, we tend to avoid managing conflict on a full–time, day–to–day basis as much as possible. To most people, conflict is always a negative force hampering their lives like misting rain. On those rare moments when we feel no stress in our relationships, we view our lives in harmony. But then something gnaws at us and we know intuitively that conflict is fermenting somewhere in our lives. Therefore, we tend to avoid conflict as much as possible ... knowing deep down conflict will never fully go away in our lives. Most people try to avoid conflict in many non-productive ways.

Fight or Flight

Fighting or fleeing conflict is the way many people perceive managing personal conflict. Often, fighting or fleeing from conflict results in not addressing basic conflict issues. These underlying issues will not resolve themselves and will continue in a state of fermentation or development. For example, if a supervisor will not hear employees explain how processing work differently will save the company money, the underlying cost issues will continue assuming the employees are correct. Fighting or overpowering employees will quickly solve a problem, but usually will not resolve the underlying issues. The supervisor can exert power over the employees and keep production procedures as they are; however, the real cost problem may only be temporarily solved. The underlying production issues of long term cost to the company remain unaddressed and ongoing. These production issues will inevitably resurface in the future when the supervisor is promoted or fired.

Quick Solution

On the other hand, a few people feel they must solve every one of their problems immediately, no matter the ultimate consequences. There is a rush to make a quick decision without considering all of the issues. Of course, in some cases, there are problems which require solving by making decisions immediately. Burial arrangements must be made quickly, no matter how painful they are to the family. Although burial arrangements are a one time decision and are affected by time pressures, there still may be lingering family issues which must be addressed. In one incident, although the deceased had asked to be cremated, his wife chose an open casket and cemetery burial. The burial decision was made by the one in power (the wife); however, the deceased's mother was very upset that her son's wishes were not granted. After the burial, there are still lingering issues of resentment. Even friends choosing a restaurant may cause a major argument or discussion if underlying issues of power are present. If one person within a group always wants his way and the group gives in because it is easier, then the underlying group power issues will never get resolved. Seemingly everyday conflicts appear superficial and incidental, and not worth much discussion. Therefore, many people cope with conflicts in ways that make them immediately go away by selecting a quick and easy solution ... such as agreeing with the other person. But many of these daily choice/conflicts are manifestations of the same underlying issues which were unattended in the last confrontation on the subject. If we honestly look at common connections between problems, we often see interrelated issues which have not been properly handled earlier. These basic issues occur over and over again because their importance was not discussed. We humans simply go through a process of changing the pictures on the wall, instead of resolving the real basis of the conflict.

Avoidance

Avoidance equals moving aside the real issue and arguing over other issues. Thus, the true conflict or problem can be avoided for the time being. My daughters would always attempt to move the real issue by turning on me for getting mad at them. Avoidance also occurs when one adopts the ideas and attitudes of the opposing party. In these cases, the individual denies a problem exists. However, avoidance undermines an individual's integrity because deep down people are not true to themselves. They fail to properly engage the conflict and they know it.

People also waste energy on problems because they move them around. They simply change the location of the problem. An employee is moved from one department to another. It appears that the initial problem is solved; however, this employee's work habits have only been hidden in a new department. The same employee's work problems crop up again, but this time there are two departments impacted and the underlying conflict and the issues have grown in the process. A relocation not only expands the original work problem, but also has the potential to cause a new charge of false merit evaluation by the new supervisor.

Chapter Two

Denial

Denial of conflict produces results similar to rearranging the problem. The problem does not go away; it only resurfaces in a stronger form. *Fear is a companion of denial when it comes to engaging conflict.* Denial of conflict only makes the conflict worse and the internalized fear greater. People play a fantasy game of "Say it and it will be so" to neutralize the fear and deny the problem. Instead of engaging problems, people say "I just won't think about it." One of the greatest examples of denial is portrayed in the book, <u>Gone With The Wind</u>. Upon being rebuffed and walked out on by Rhett Butler, Scarlett O'Hara states, *"I'll think about that tomorrow."* This game reaches it climax when parents completely sidestep the issue of their child's insecurity about their looks as an adolescent. The parents say, "You are beautiful to us" or "you are not fat to us." Such statements, although well meaning by the parents, teach denial as a manner of dealing with personal internal conflict and growth. Another parental power game is the "we will fix it" game. Many parents teach children that others will fix their conflicts. The lawyer will fix the speeding ticket or accident. Money or influence will fix the problem. These power games teach the lesson that if one has enough of the right power any conflict can be fixed. The denial aspect of these power games is that the real issues creating the conflict do not have to be addressed. The true issues creating fear and distress can be denied because they are anticipated to go away.

For those individuals who feel they have no personal power, denial can mask a fear of personal face–to–face interaction. Individuals often feel safer interacting through the internet rather than with people one–on–one. The internet buffers reactions and provides a protective shield. Questions do not have to be answered in a vulnerable, face–to–face interaction. One's identify can be coded. It is remarkable that the internet opens up the world, yet its current communication process insulates individuals and decreases valuable communication skills. Sound bites replace meaningful and full communication. Valuable dialogue, which fosters and builds relationships through full exploration of issues, true meaning and understanding, is often lost in cyberspace.

Rationalization

Rationalization is another common way for individuals to avoid conflict. Rationalizing involves mentally deciding to analytically manipulate the situation or desired resolution to avoid facing the central issues. The individual can thus successfully avoid facing the underlying problems that, at some point, must be addressed to engage and resolve the conflict. For example, an employee might say, "Oh, well, I wouldn't have gotten the raise anyway", when his annual review was not as good as expected. Instead of questioning the unfavorable issues with his boss, the employee just backs away and rationalizes the conflict with his evaluation. Many people will avoid issues or people by simply disassociating with or detaching from the conflict. While this behavior may have short term results, the long range effect is to allow the problem to ferment and become more potent.

Tunnel Vision and Rigid Attitude

Tunnel vision, or only seeing a limited range of possibilities, combined with a rigid attitude is another highly destructive pattern of avoiding conflict. Avoidance differs from tunnel vision and rigid attitudes because here the main issues are in focus with both parties. Positional bargaining on the issue, due to rigid attitudes and tunnel vision, causes excessive anxiety within the individual and creates more tension and fear as to the result of the confrontation. These defenses are often subconscious, and individuals do not realize they are harming themselves by not being open to other values or beliefs. I know of a family situation where the parents have very rigid attitudes about their children respecting their every wish ... even as grown and married children. The daughter does as her parents desire, yet the son resents the control and has not communicated with his parents or sister in several years. There is great stress within the family, but neither the son nor the father will even discuss the values which cause them to disagree ... each knowing they are correct in their own position. No amount of discussion will change their minds! Heavy investment in particular values are typical of this conflict. People will invest their attitudes, beliefs, resources, skills, techniques and defenses into a certain position or stake. Giving these values up in the process of conflict resolution would cause them to lose face and self esteem. Therefore, they maintain their position at all cost. For example, consider many issues of race, gender, or sex. In these situations, conflict continues because many people choose to invest in their out–of–date values.

Past Experience

All too often individuals will not view conflict with clear reality of the facts, but rather through how they have dealt with conflict in the past. Thus the present conflict will be managed with old skills. The conflict presents real life issues that need to be addressed. However, the real issues are masked and the solutions are biased based upon the limits of the person's past experiences. Any solution will almost become a self–fulfilling prophecy. Certainly, the outcomes will only be shaped by preconceived solutions and not currently mediated resolutions. A wife in divorce mediation may not sell or move out of her house because psychologically she feels that she will be an outcast among her peer group. Even though she can't afford to maintain the house, she will stay. Finally she may be forced to sell the house making her self–fulfilling prophecy of being an outcast come true.

Excessive Involvement

On the flip side, another behavior is excessive involvement in a conflict. Some individuals seek conflict because it reassures them they are not afraid. They will become energized and fight to prove themselves equal to the conflict. Such aggressive behavior is meant to disguise their fear of low personal power or another's greater power. Welcoming a fight is not healthy. That behavior is like seeking a disease.

Conflict Alienates People

Of all the atrocities in the world today, none compare to a person's isolation or separation from his own spirit, other individuals, a spiritual power, or God. Separation or isolation for whatever cause (whether forced from outside sources or from within), leads to behavior that alienates. Alienation divides people and nations because of idolatrous thinking which thereby inhibits peaceful relationships. Without proper relationships that tie individuals to acceptable social norms, people act on their own and as they choose. Gang or terrorist behavior is a good example os social norm rejection. Gangs or terrorist cells attract isolated and separated individuals. Individuals detach from traditional values of religious or social norms. Since gang or terrorist behavior is not tied to acceptable social norms, gang members are free to behave as they choose outside the normal social norms that hold society together.

History records copious stories of relational splits, not only with individuals and nations, but also with the Divine. Such stories and myths represent the collective culture and demonstrate to successive generations the way the world works. Myth and stories, recorded as history, become fact. Fact becomes today's struggle, presenting itself again and again as conflict that is proper in our world. Thus, cultural norms are established. The society and its culture feeds off this collective conflict without any thought of learning lessons from these episodes of human isolation and pain.

When there is a collective example of conflict denial, power replaces learning as a process to deal with the consequences of collective conflict. Individuals and nations use various power techniques. Employing such techniques cause non–relational thinking. Use of the power paradigm separates individual from individual, and nation from nation. Spirals of conflict emerge and rise as increasing power is needed. Power keeps escalating. Conflict loops back to crush individuals and nations in its wake. Wave after wave of collective conflict engulfs civilization like a storm's tidal wave. Terrorists nurture and feed themselves on this rich fodder of fear. Nourishment of world conflict flourishes to feed a spreading fear of future destruction and isolation.

Conflict's Positive Side

Immunization from conflict is non–existent. Accept this fact! Also realize conflict has a positive side. Conflict has positive aspects which can enhance the character of our lives. One of the advantages of conflict is the prevention of stagnation. Another advantage to conflict is that it stimulates interest and curiosity. A third advantage is that it can bring about personal and social change. A fourth advantage to conflict is that it helps define groups and individuals.

The positive side, with corresponding good results, manifests itself when conflict is properly engaged at the earliest point in its growth. This engagement is the start of a management process that allows the conflict to play out in a healthy way because it is contained within a workable system of resolution. Thus, conflict can be a positive force in our lives and produce positive results.

The real difference in whether conflict turns negative or positive depends upon how people perceive, engage, and manage their conflict on an ongoing basis. Conflict inappropriately handled causes tremendous stress in our lives. Conflict managed properly can enhance our emotional, intellectual and moral qualities and transforms our nature and make–up in a positive way.

Let's look at an example of properly engaging conflict and separating personal blame from the conflict. At a non–profit board meeting, board members bristled when one member overshot the budget on mailers to members. Disgusted board members kibitzed behind closed doors and over the telephone to avoid a public fight. This situation represents a typical "fermenting" conflict. For various political reasons, board members wanted to avoid a public discussion of the problem. However, to prevent the conflict from growing, engagement of the conflict must happen.

The first step in engagement is to recognize that a conflict exists, and then to mentally separate the Board member from the problem. Therefore, at the next meeting, the Board can concentrate on the resolution rather than placing personal blame. It is decided the mailing fees can be applied to many budget areas and come within the Board's authorization limits. The board now sees how, with the proper engagement technique, conflict can be openly discussed without the negative repercussions of blame and talking behind others' backs. A positive learning experience has been created.

Properly managing conflict yields positive outcomes even though you might not always get all you want in a particular situation. Simply working a proven process will make you feel more in control of your conflict despite the immediate outcome. For instance, in business or family situations where points of view differ, expressing your perspective effectively and having it heard is powerful in itself, even if no immediate change occurs. I remember one employee saying that just telling her boss what was really distressing to her at work made her feel much better and more in control of her work life. Also, spouses who can truly express their concerns to one another feel relief and satisfaction that the air has been cleared regardless of whether a change is made immediately to resolve the problem. The saying, "I just have to get this off my chest," has real, positive meaning here as long as the process for expression is appropriate.

Engaging Conflict

Accepting conflict's ongoing nature, plus recognizing that it can have positive results, is not enough. You must 1) decide how to effectively engage conflict, 2) to follow a system, and 3) acquire the skills necessary to work the system. Then you can approach conflict with management and resolution skills rather than using the various avoidance techniques.

By now you may admit that conflict is fermenting at home or at work. You expect conflict to develop and hit you any day. In this case, conflict is like a hard–ball thrown at you at ninety miles an hour. But you have choices. You can duck or deflect the ball, or you can catch the ball. Ducking or ignoring engaging conflict only protects you for so long, and it doesn't work with all throws. Most people choose to deflect ... however, in that action they lose control of the ball. But by having a mitt, cupping their hands and catching the ball, they take immediate control. Once in control, they can redirect the ball and its force to the appropriate place. You can do the same when properly engaging conflict.

Many people recognize the truth in engaging and dealing with their problems head–on, but still defer or avoid their problems due to their lack of training in conflict management. Because we live in a world where conflict never appears to stop, some feel it is too exhausting to even consider learning to deal with it properly. Since there seems to be no effective way to win over conflict every time, many people give up and think it's easier to not even try to manage it. The old adage, "ignore it and it will go away," doesn't apply to conflict that has a serious impact on your life. Unattended conflict seeks other methods of exposure and will escalate to outright war unless it is properly engaged. Better conflict theory and practice speaks to engaging conflict as early as possible for positive results.

We need to find the proper methods of self-intervention and the proper environment in which to work on our conflict. We do not want to sit on our anger too long or we may self-destruct. We need to learn how to deal with conflict in a manner which will allow nonviolent assertiveness. Conflict will not go away; therefore, it must be managed properly for our own good.

Working a proven engagement process like the V.A.L.U.E. System will help clear your thinking. Just discussing a controversy using a logical and rational process provides clarity. As you emote out loud, you really *hear* what you are saying (and what the other person is saying), probably for the first time. By hearing this new information, both parties gain different perspectives and can ask new questions. The V.A.L.U.E. System helps refine and recycle information, thus gaining clarity. For example, if I can get people to sit together and really talk, listen, and hear each other, it is amazing how fast they will ask the right questions to get new information on the table to resolve their issues. Keep in mind that it is the non-talk with all the hidden meanings and assumptions that keeps a conflict growing until it is too late.

> **KEY POINT**
>
> Resolving a conflict based upon old information is very difficult, as there is nothing new to work with toward resolution.

Most importantly, when you use an organized system to confront conflict, you model rational behavior to others. In turn, others will see you as responding to conflict less offensively. The other party will likely feel less defensive and will react in a like manner because he/she feels less threatened and wants to appear rational. Such a start is the open door to the positive side of conflict management.

Another large benefit of properly engaging conflict is the reduction of fear associated with conflict. This fear of losing incubates worry and anxiety. Conflicts become fear-driven instead of communication-and-issue-driven. When this dynamic happens, the power of fear overrides logic or clarity and outcomes are rarely positive. Remember that the force of a conflict can have a positive or negative effect depending on how you "catch" or handle the force. Knowing how to deal with conflict reduces your fears, allows you to properly assess a situation from many sides, and fosters a rational decision making attitude. Having such an attitude strengthens your emotional, intellectual, and moral well–being because you become confident of your ability to engage conflict. You also reduce your stress level.

I deal with many students who cannot see or hear a logical solution because they are projecting fear into their legal conflicts. Their minds freeze with fear and rational thinking halts. They feel totally out of control with no available options. My job demands I put them back in control of their legal issues. Using a step–by–step process to actively engage them in their legal conflict is worth the time and effort. Conflict engagement as an intervention strategy works because students then feel in control of their life. They engage in conflict with my help and validation.

Maintaining control through a proven process, whether diet, exercise, or conflict engagement, enhances self–esteem. Improved self–esteem boosts productivity, lessens worry, lowers stress, and produces a better mental and physical condition. Thus, properly managing conflict enhances your emotional, intellectual, and moral well–being and positively transforms you into a more productive, happier person.

Chapter Two

How To Manage Conflict Effectively

We all want value in our lives, although much of the time we feel empty in our relationships with others. Too often, individuals go through life seeking value in relationships yet getting no benefit in return. Therefore people lose interest in existing relationships and find no motivation for developing new ones. If existing relationships turn into conflict, they deteriorate rapidly because no one teaches us skills to "value" other individuals in order to preserve good relationships. Most people do want to keep their relationships, but need to learn how to work with conflict within their relationships. Keeping the following concepts of V.A.L.U.E. in mind will allow any conflict to take its proper place in our thinking, and at the same time preserve the integrity of all involved in the relationship. Preserving relationships through the V.A.L.U.E. System sends a clear message that you value who and what the other person is, thus encouraging proper conflict resolution actions in the future.

The V.A.L.U.E. System works because it is based on sound conflict resolution experience field tested in actual practice, in addition to being used in mediations and other forms of dispute resolution. Experienced mediators are good communicators and apply skills like the ones in the V.A.L.U.E. System. The V.A.L.U.E. System also works on the practical, human philosophy that people have more of a desire to have their needs and wants seen, felt, and heard than the need to always be right, 100% of the time. All of us want to feel we have the right to be seen and heard, and our presence felt without being discounted. The V.A.L.U.E. System accomplishes this goal.

Chapter Three

If war is the violent resolution of conflict, then peace is not the absence of conflict, but rather, the ability to resolve conflict without violence.
C. T. Lawrence Butler

THE V.A.L.U.E. SYSTEM

Benefits of the V.A.L.U.E. System

V.A.L.U.E. stands for Validation, Add, Learn, Understand, and Empower. Each are communication blocks for resolution of conflict. Each block is a step in the process. To derive the maximum benefits from the V.A.L.U.E. System, at least one person needs to utilize the V.A.L.U.E. System. The acronym V.A.L.U.E. is easy to remember because everyone wants value in his life. Validation means to assure another person he/she has been fully heard, and acknowledges her as a person along with her ideas. Add means to validate the other person's perception while also including your perception in addition to theirs. Learn refers to a process of defining the substance of conflict issues. Understand means to contrast the distinctions and differences between two conflict concepts or issues and to explore and develop the substance of the differences for resolution. Empower allows the formation of options from the Understand block and the creation of an Empowerment Plan.

The V.A.L.U.E. System is like a plexiglass shield. It allows one to engage conflict without fear. In prisons housing dangerous inmates, the guards use plexiglass shields on rollers to protect themselves from harmful objects the prisoners secretly made and might throw at them. At the same time, the clear shield allows the guards a full view of the inmates. This system allows guards a safe method of checking on the prisoners without getting hurt. By analogy, the V.A.L.U.E. System permits you to see conflict and begin to engage it without getting hurt in the process. The V.A.L.U.E. System acts like a shield to help you manage your conflicts properly.

Recycle Personal Conflicts

Recycling, in the communication process of the V.A.L.U.E. system, means to take the other person's perspective and add yours for dialogue. Mixing perspectives with discussion allows a recycled view of the conflict.

After learning to utilize the V.A.L.U.E. System, you will be able to recycle your personal conflicts in a more positive fashion, maintaining your individual identity and integrity. Mary is a good example. From past conflict experiences, Mary learned that engaging conflict depreciated her as a person. Every time she disclosed her ideas she was criticized as a bleeding-heart liberal. However using the V.A.L.U.E. System, Mary is now confident in adding her point of view. She maintains her own integrity with her own unique perspective on social issues. Now she can say, "Yes, your views are such and such and my views are these." She gets to state her views because she is not fighting her friends' views. Mary is acknowledging the views of others and then adding her own.

Enhance Relationships

Your relationships with others will be enhanced because the V.A.L.U.E. System permits people with whom you are in conflict to be who they are, faults and all. No one has to surrender her individual identity in order to engage the conflict. Honor for others is built into the V.A.L.U.E. System; thus, using the system gains mutual respect. Bruce is having a difficult time negotiating a commercial lease with some Generation X leasing managers. He hails from the old school of 'coat and tie' while the lease managers dress casually. For Bruce, proper office dress equals respect. Fortunately, Bruce validated in his mind that acceptable office dress in 2009 can be more casual. Thus, he could continue to negotiate with these "kids" and feel respected. Due to his new attitude (shown by his non-verbal behavior) the "kids" in turn showed him the respect he needed in other ways. Bruce made the deal he wanted.

No Fight or Flight Attitude

Using the V.A.L.U.E. System, one no longer has to fight or to escape. Perhaps you have a problem with your employer over tardiness due to your being a single parent. The V.A.L.U.E. System allows you to deal with such problems in a logical and business like fashion without either party feeling compromised. In other words, you can still be heard without jeopardizing your job. The V.A.L.U.E. System may even increase your rapport with your boss based upon your new approach to the problem. For example, if your boss wants you at work on time everyday, she may express anger with you for your tardiness. Using the V.A.L.U.E. System you can begin to demonstrate respect for your boss's work policies by letting her know you acknowledge the policies, even though you may have a personal problem strictly following them. You will learn to discuss the issues underlying your situation as a single mother from a resolution point of view, rather than from a "fix–it" perspective. Therefore, cool minds can explore resolution options such as flex–time and not focus on blame or power issues.

Maintain Control of Conflict

Applying the V.A.L.U.E. System will help you to remain in control of conflict. By confidently engaging problems head–on, you will be able to transform a stressful situation into something manageable. The stress of conflict occurs when one feels she can't manage the fight that inevitably happens when the conflict gets out of control and

Chapter Three

escalates. Mary is mentally quick and analyzes issues fast. As a precocious child she attempted to express her views of a conflict, opposing her parents' views. But her parents would spin the discussion on to another topic – her "bad behavior" – then start blaming her for the conflict. She always felt hurt in this process. Mary now follows a step–by–step process to keep her parents on course. She can now express her views, while also learning her parents' views as well. Both parents and daughter are now able to understand each other because they follow the steps of the V.A.L.U.E. System.

Manage and Move On

The System allows you to follow a set process to manage problems. Once you have done all you can, you are able to forget the incident and move on, regardless of the outcome. Although the results will be overwhelmingly favorable to one working the system, positive results may not transpire immediately. Why? Others may not be ready to resolve the conflict within that particular timeframe. However, others get *new information* during this process, and by taking time to think about this *new information* on their own, they can resolve the conflict with you at a later time. A family quarrel is a typical example because spouses and children are at different places during a conflict. By giving others time to think about new information that is revealed, they can process the new information and resolve the issues in their mind in a more timely manner. Mary now allows her parents time to process her new information instead of forcing them to make a quick decision. Her parents can say, "Now that we have thought about this new information, we can do such and such." Mary is also more tolerant of people that don't process information as quickly as she does. Mary previously thought people were just being difficult. Now she looks at differences in peoples' processing speeds and validates this fact. This recognition in turn keeps her on track, whether she is managing personal or business conflict.

New Skills for Old Problems

You will discover new skills for handling old problems. Old problems never go away; they just resurface in other forms. However, the V.A.L.U.E. System allows you to pull apart the old problem into pieces and work on each piece separately. Every problem is made up of several issues. The V.A.L.U.E. System allows all parties to explore their feelings about the differences in the issues. Understanding these differences equals new information, and in turn, new information allows old problems to be resolved. Like in Mary's case, people will say, "Oh, knowing this new information, I can now do such and such, and I think that will resolve the problem."

Recognize Conflict Earlier

You will learn to recognize conflict earlier so you can deal with the situation to protect yourself from unnecessary hurt. Remember Mary? She was always quick to analyze a problem, break it into parts and find a resolution. But her parents were not that quick-minded, and she always felt hurt from early engagement in the conflict. Mary can now engage conflict when she recognizes it growing because she

Chapter Three

uses a process to manage the discussion and timing. Mary has studied the pathology of conflict in Chapter II. Now she can recognize the stage of her current conflict, add her views, learn her parents' views, and understand differences in these views. Finally, when the time is right, she may offer suggestions for resolution. Most importantly, what Mary knows and what others will discover through the V.A.L.U.E. System is one can face conflict and still have your needs met. The V.A.L.U.E. System leaves all parties whole and protected in the process. The process produces mutual honor, learning, and understanding of differences in order to foster resolution. Many negotiators point out that it takes compromise or mutual agreement to resolve conflict. This book takes a completely different approach.

KEY POINT

The V.A.L.U.E. System posits that validating others and their perspectives, discovering and discussing differences, not commonalities, resolves conflict. The V.A.L.U.E. System is based upon a process to uncover and learn others' differences, then explore and understand these differences in order to expose new information. Once this new information is discovered, people have new reason to resolve their problems with others. Both parties may not like what they see, hear or feel; however, they can live with the resolution because they know and finally understand each other's perspective.

The V.A.L.U.E. Process

The V.A.L.U.E. System is an organized process to properly engage and manage conflict. As described in Chapter III, there are five easy blocks to follow. Each block puts you closer to resolution of your personal or business conflict. Keep in mind the order of the blocks is important. Follow each block in its entirety before going on to the next block. The proper order is a key to the system's success, because each block builds upon the preceding one. Diagram I shows the blocks in their proper building order, and the concept within each block.

BUILDING BLOCKS OF THE V.A.L.U.E. SYSTEM

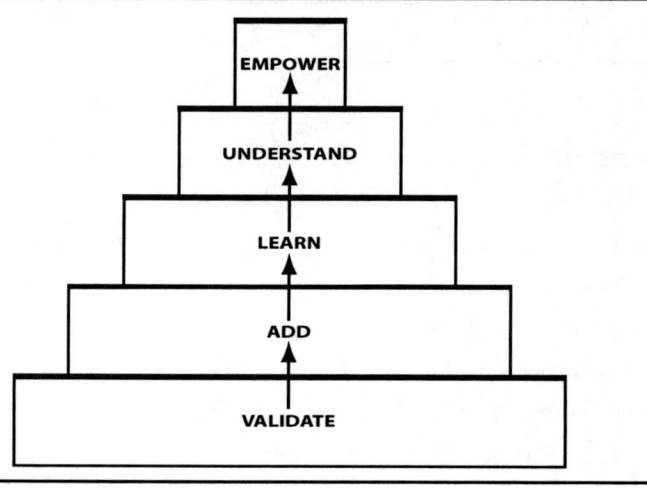

```
                    EMPOWER
                       ↑
                  UNDERSTAND
                       ↑
                     LEARN
                       ↑
                      ADD
                       ↑
                   VALIDATE
```

Diagram I – Building Blocks of the V.A.L.U.E. System

Once you learn the building process, the necessary communication process will become second nature to you and you will be able to build to a resolution quickly. You

Chapter Three

can also adapt the system to your style of communication as long as your language is similar to the key words and phrases that are so important. They're outlined for you in the following chapters, and the V.A.L.U.E. guide in Chapter IX.

This book should be used as a communication guide and process tool for conflict resolution in your life. Accordingly, take your time to learn each educational block without rushing through the chapter. Read a learning block and apply the concepts and words of that section to your daily dealings. Become completely comfortable with one block before moving on to the next. Experiment with each tool and make notes of how well it worked. Go back and re-read the block and compare your notes with the chapter concepts, key words, and phrases. The more you use these key words and phrases the more comfortable you will become. With practice the key phrases will become second nature to you. Don't worry if at first the key words and phrases sound strange or you think you are repetitious at times. Those you communicate with will sense a change; but they will also sense that it is easier to talk with you ... especially if you are validating them or their ideas. If, as you proceed through the process, the other party is not cooperative within a particular block, remember to go back and validate the person for their ideas, values, or beliefs. In Diagram I you see that Validation is the foundation block of the entire process. Validation needs to be present at each stage of the process. You will also know if a particular block is working because all of the necessary information was given to complete that block of the system.

How the V.A.L.U.E. Process Works

Five easy building blocks comprise the V.A.L.U.E. system. A brief explanation of the blocks follows so you can see how each block fits together easily. I need to emphasize that validation needs to be utilized throughout each block to show the other person that you are willing to allow them to express themselves and be heard. Therefore, let's start with Validation.

Validation

First, validation does not equal agreement with the other side's argument! You can validate a person or their ideas without agreeing with them. Validation is a communication tool that allows other people to present themselves as they are in conflict, warts and all. Their ideas, beliefs, and values, which are in conflict with yours, are acknowledged. Validation says in essence, "I will let you personally be who you are right now in our conflict. I will let you tell me your ideas, perceptions, values or beliefs as you see them right now. I will not judge you or your ideas. I will hear you and in turn communicate to you that I have heard you and your ideas. I will not try to change you or your ideas at the present time, yet

Chapter Three

I reserve the right not to agree with them completely. Validation can be as simple as, "I hear (see or feel) you say ... then repeating exactly what the other person said. For example, "I hear you say you are very angry."

ADD

Once the other person and his views have been effectively validated, you are now in a position to *add* your own views. The method of adding your views is critical. We want to add our perspective without depreciating the value of others. If we say, "Yes, I understand *but* my views are this", we discount the other person's views by using the word "but". This *"yes, but"* communication negates the person's perspective instead of honoring his beliefs as previously validated. The technique to add your views does just that – it adds without disregarding the other person's views. Simply state, "I hear your views are such and such AND I would like to add mine. My perspective is such and such." This language leaves the other person and his views whole. Therefore, through mutual respect your views may be added to the total mix of perspectives.

LEARN

Once all perspectives are on the table through the ADD process, it is time to *learn* what these other perspectives really mean. Normally perspective, beliefs or values are broad concepts like love, hate, independence, or fairness. Such perspectives give a direction, but not a map of what they really mean to the other person. Learn means asking for the belief, value, or perspective to be defined for you. Break each perspective into three parts (maximum) for a definition of its meaning. Diagram II shows how this works with the concept of "employment fairness."

AN EMPLOYEE'S PERSPECTIVE OF "EMPLOYMENT FAIRNESS"

(Pie chart with three sections: Equal Opportunity, Just Compensation, An Honest Company Policy)

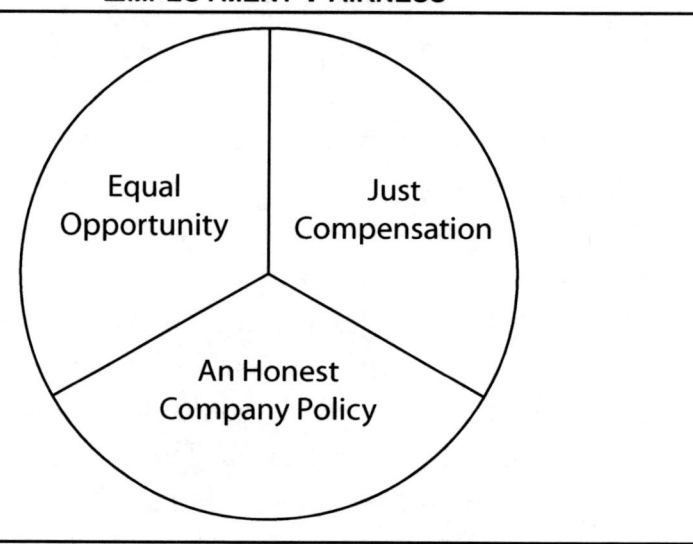

Diagram II – An Employee's Perspective of "Employment Fairness"

Thus, to one employee the idea of employment fairness equals three main ingredients; (1) equal opportunity, (2) just compensation, and (3) an honest company policy.

Chapter Three

UNDERSTAND

Understand means to explore in depth the differences and distinctions of each person's perspective on each issue. At this time in the conflict, similarities are not causing a conflict; therefore, there is no need to explore these issues within this block. Understanding the perceptual differences and their meaning present the best opportunity for resolution. In our previous example, once we know for sure how the employee defines fairness in his employment situation we can begin to understand why there may be a conflict. Why? Because the employer's definition may be different from the employee's in one or more of the three ingredients illustrated above. For example, the employer may agree with (1) equal opportunity and (3) and honest company policy, yet not #2 ("just compensation"). This term may be too broad in scope for the employer, or the company may have been sued over compensation issues. Therefore, the next step is to understand the differences in "just compensation" as there is no conflict with the other parts of the employment fairness issue. Within the discussion, new information will come out that was not known before. Diagram III below shows how this discussion looks set out side to side for comparison of the "just compensation" issue.

"Just Compensation"

Employee	Employer
1. Work performed to specifications.	1. Work performed accurately.
2. Hourly pay up to 40 hours a week.	2. Work performed in a timely manner.
3. Overtime pay above 40 hours a week.	3. No overtime pay for production lags.

Diagram III – Just Compensation

From this diagram of the "just compensation" issue, the employer and employee easily see the real difference boils down to overtime pay, and specifically to the timing of the overtime pay. Both parties now understand this difference as new information not disclosed before the discussions.

Empowerment

The Empowerment block consists of working on the latest new information to produce options for resolution of the conflict. With new information on the table, the parties are empowered to think of options to resolve this conflict. Some options may have surfaced in the Understand block. Such options can be discussed in the Empowerment block. For Example, the options in Diagram IV could be put on the negotiation table.

Win / Win Options

Employee	Employer
1. Employee is not responsible for mechanical line delays. 2. Production line delays will be counted as overtime pay for employees.	1. The company will service line equipment better and faster. 2. Employee can choose flex–time in lieu of overtime pay for line delays.

Diagram IV – Win / Win Options

Perhaps, with the above options available and on the table, the employee could say, "Now that I know the company will service the line equipment better and faster, if there is overtime I can take it in the form of flex–time, not overtime pay." Of course there could be other options; these are examples only. The point is, once we specifically define what the perceptual differences are and discuss these distinctions, new information surfaces. With new information people can see new options for themselves and new ways to negotiate a resolution. They can save face by saying, "Knowing this new information, I can agree to these terms."

Once resolution is reached under this V.A.L.U.E. system, the agreement lasts because the true underlying issues and concerns were discovered and discussed in detail. In this example there was no need to compromise on the issues because both parties received what they needed in the process ... a resolution based upon their definition of employment fairness.

The V.A.L.U.E. system can be used at any stage in the growth of conflict. However, the sooner one engages conflict the better the outcome for all involved. Once a conflict parses the confrontation stage and reaches the violent stage, true skill is required to validate and acknowledge the parties enough for each to sit down and discuss differences. Engaging conflict in the fermentation, awareness, or early confrontation stage is best. At these stages, the parties are more open to proper engagement and dialogue.

The more one integrates the knowledge of how conflict grows with the V.A.L.U.E. system, the more one begins to engage conflict at an earlier stage. Confidence in one's ability to engage and manage conflict through the V.A.L.U.E. system prevents a fear of engagement. Therefore, you will not be afraid to "sense" a conflict brewing and properly engage it.

Communications Issues

The concepts, words, and phrases that make this communication system operate at full potential need to be stated in the proper tone of voice. According to most books on communication, tonality in communication plays a bigger role than most people realize. Diagram V below shows what a large factor tonality plays in communication. Tonality accounts for at least 70% of all communication (*Human Behavior in Business*), and determines how ideas are received by the other person.

COMPONENTS OF COMMUNICATION

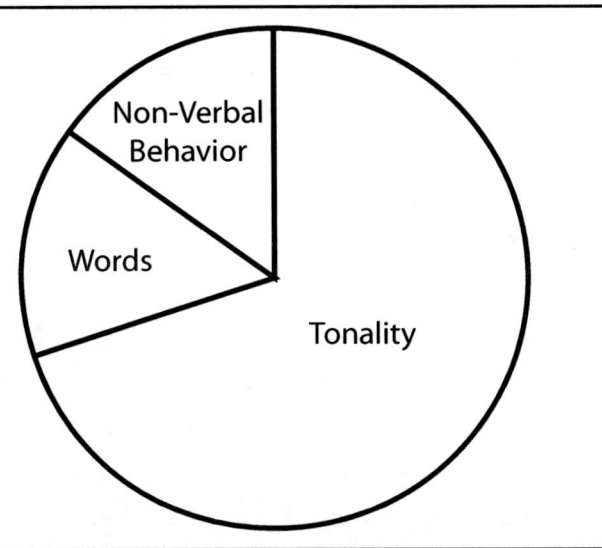

Diagram V – Components of Communication

As important as words are, how one says them – the tone encompassing the word – is even more important. Take a simple phrase like, "I could just kill him." Such a phrase could have many meanings depending upon how it was said. The speaker could be very literal and mean that she had formed an intent to murder another man. On the other hand, the speaker could only be using a common phrase to mean the other person said or did something she didn't like. Therefore, they were just mad or irritated with the speaker. The difference in tonality can determine the meaning. A light tonality would indicate just irritation. A heavy, dark, and menacing tonality would indicate intent to do physical harm to the other person. Another example is sarcasm. "Yea, sure" can mean agreement or complete rejection in contemporary communications, depending upon tonality of voice.

    Another example of a communication problem is sounding patronizing (like you are responding parent to child), especially when one adds a little sarcasm. To avoid a patronizing tonality, use a very neutral tone of voice without any element of judgment creeping into the words. Often, patronizing conversations have judgmental tones built into them. Avoid this tonality at all cost! Simply state the other person's beliefs or values in a neutral tone without your perspective or judgment attached. A statement like, "I don't want to be married to you anymore" is hard to accept. The response can be patronizing like, "I'm not stupid ... I've known you were unhappy with me for a long time." This type of response demonstrates an attitude of superiority and a judgment call on the responder's part. However, a neutral response would be, "I hear you don't want to be married to me anymore. Can we talk about it?" No arrogance or judgment call exists in the last response ... only a neutral repetition of exactly what the person said and a request for more information through dialogue. This technique is like looking in a mirror – you repeat what you see without adding any editorial comments.

    The non–verbal aspect of communication also plays a vital part in interactions. It is often said that our actions speak louder than our words. When we act differently than what we say, the other person senses that we are not authentic or congruent in our communication. If you say "yes" to a proposal, yet your arms are crossed over your chest and your face is bright red, the other person really has a difficult time believing you are serious with your acceptance. You say "yes", but look and act like you mean "no." Paying attention to these communication issues will greatly enhance your effectiveness with the system's operation. Focused attention makes you a much better communicator. You will also be better at resolving conflict.

Let's Get Started

In the following chapters we will begin a specific exploration of each building block of the V.A.L.U.E. system. You will learn (1) the reason for the process, (2) the process in detail, (3) words, phrases or techniques to employ at each stage, and (4) review real life examples which demonstrate the correct process at each stage. Again, don't rush through these chapters. Study them and apply them to your daily life. Keep trying and don't give up on yourself. It takes a little time to learn anything new. Be patient with yourself in working this system as the rewards will be worth the practicing and learning experience. Good reading and good luck!

Seeing Through The Wall

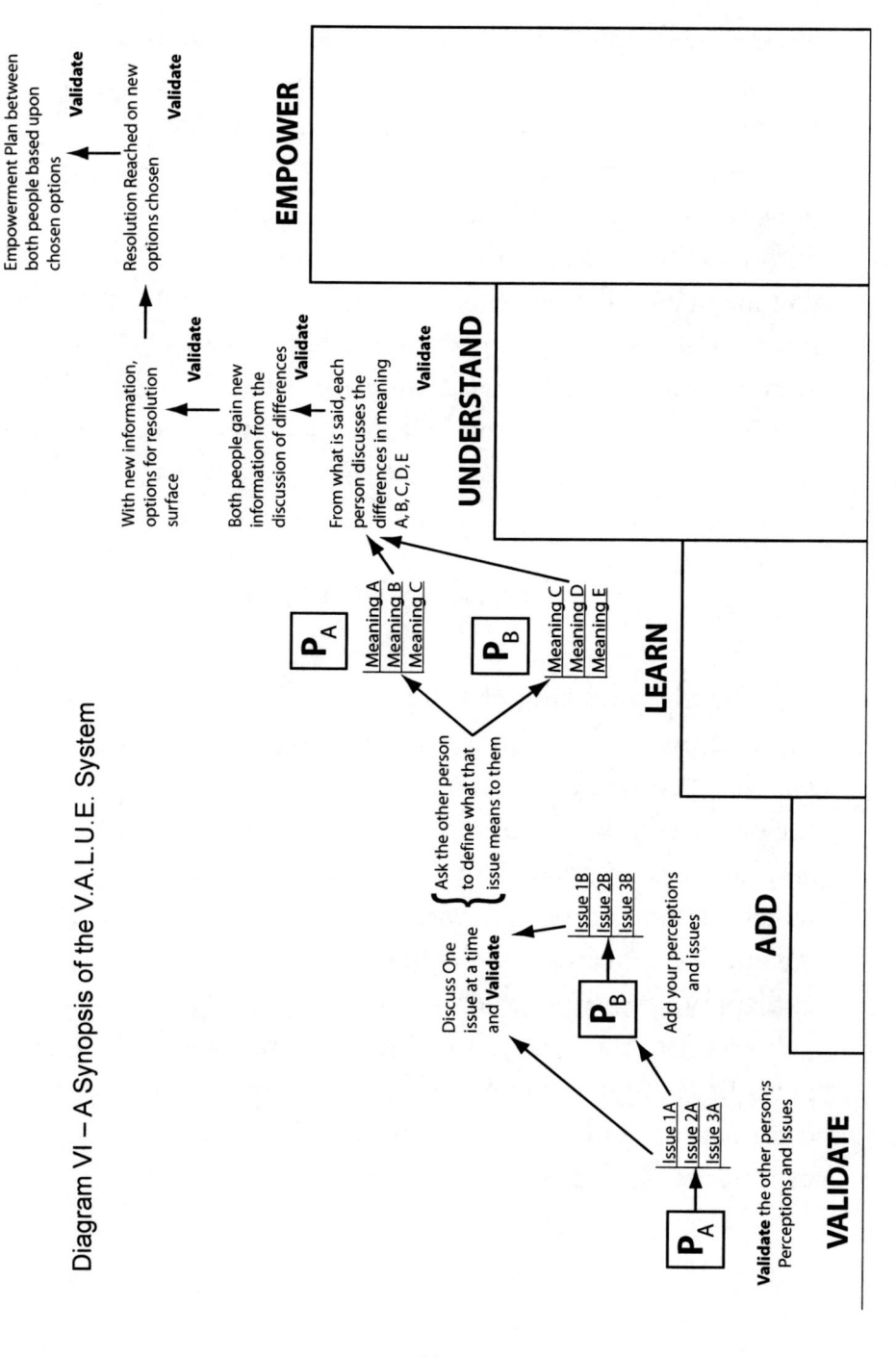

Diagram VI – A Synopsis of the V.A.L.U.E. System

EMPOWER

Empowerment Plan between both people based upon chosen options — **Validate**

Resolution Reached on new options chosen — **Validate**

With new information, options for resolution surface — **Validate**

Both people gain new information from the discussion of differences — **Validate**

From what is said, each person discusses the differences in meaning A, B, C, D, E — **Validate**

UNDERSTAND

P_A Meaning A / Meaning B / Meaning C

P_B Meaning C / Meaning D / Meaning E

LEARN

Ask the other person to define what that issue means to them

Discuss One issue at a time and **Validate**

P_B Issue 1B / Issue 2B / Issue 3B

Add your perceptions and issues

ADD

P_A Issue 1A / Issue 2A / Issue 3A

Validate the other person;s Perceptions and Issues

VALIDATE

64

Chapter Four

To understand what another person is saying, you must assume that it is true and try to imagine what it could be true of.
George Miller
Princeton's James S. McDonnell Distinguished University Professor of Psychology, Emeritus

V.A.L.U.E. BLOCK ONE: VALIDATION

WHAT IS VALIDATION?

Validation is a communication process and not an end result. Validating means to verify a person's right to her perspective on a conflict at the present moment.

Validating a person, his ideas, or his position constitutes a multidimensional process. Diagram VII below shows various aspects of a person that validation touches.

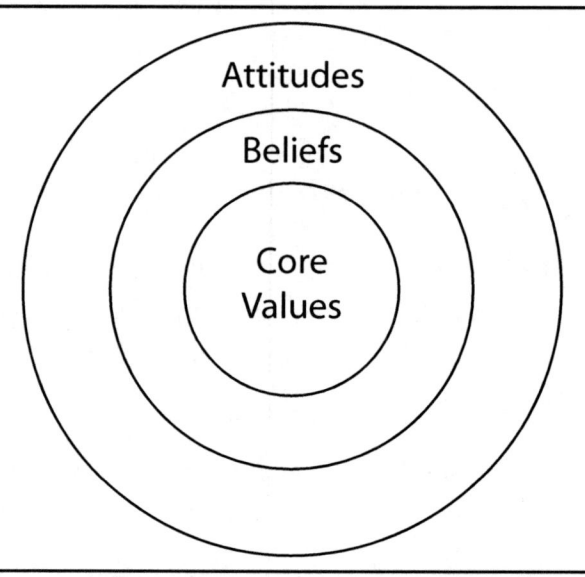

Diagram VII – Validation Touches Many Aspects of a Person

Deep in the core of a person are her values or value system. Religious value would be a good example of this concept. Sometimes these core values are hard to discover because they are not often talked about or seen in action. Beliefs are based upon the individual's values and may be more visible. For example, a religious conservative may have a belief about abortion based upon her religious values. Let's label this belief anti–abortion. One may see or hear this belief stated as a position a person takes in her life expressed as an attitude. An attitude is seen on the surface of people in the way they express themselves, what they verbalize, and their actions. For the anti–abortionist an attitude would be expressed by picketing an abortion clinic or voting for a political candidate who opposes abortion.

Thus, when people express themselves we may only recognize the outward shell or their attitude. For example, if we see a woman picketing in front of a medical clinic with anti–abortion signs, we know her position on abortion. To be sure of her beliefs and values we would have to ask her specifically what they were on this issue.

Proper validation would sound like this, "I see you are peacefully picketing with anti–abortion signs in front of Dr. X's office. Can we discuss your beliefs and values on abortion in more detail?" This validation acknowledges, in a factual manner, the behavior and the position of the picketer in a neutral, non–threatening manner. It also asks for a dialogue or disclosure of her beliefs and values on abortion. This dialogue can come later.

Again, the process of validating means to verify a person's right to look, feel, think, talk, and behave like they are doing at the present moment. For most beginners, the process of validating another individual, especially in a dispute situation, is counter–intuitive or opposite of what they think should happen. Beginners think: why reward 'bad' behavior, language, particular thinking or a particular position? The answer is one is only validating a right to communicate these ideas or behavior in a free society —not agreeing with the specific behavior, feeling, thinking, or position. The importance of this last statement is critical to the concept. Again, validation does not equal agreement!

Validation and agreement speak to different purposes. Valuing others does not mean that I like their position, behavioral characteristics, ideas, or values. It means they, at present, possess their own position, characteristics, ideas, or values and I recognize these as a fact in our conflict. Therefore, I will state these facts to the other person so they know I feel such facts are present in our conflict. This open recognition also prevents me from making critical comments or judgments about their behavior, values, or ideas. By this technique, I am simply making a statement of fact concerning the other person while preventing my personal values or judgments to get in the middle of the conflict. Think of the people you often call to talk with, eat lunch with, or with whom you go to special events. I'll bet these acquaintances may not always agree with you; however, they allow you to act, behave, and express yourself in your own special style. Of course they do or you would not like them. In turn, you validate them in the same manner.

By validating, we leave people intact and therefore able to communicate with each other because they don't feel a need to be defensive. Many people feel that by recognizing the other person's ideas or characteristics, they give up their own beliefs and depreciate themselves in the process. Nothing could be farther from the truth. Recognizing the other person as whole also allows us to get our own self–recognition. "Valuing" is a two way street. Even if the validation turns out to be one–way or one–sided, the validation process still allows the validator to stay whole and not surrender his values in the process of conflict.

The dynamic of validation appears to be magic because today hardly anyone is allowed to "be" in conflict. What does it mean to "be" in conflict? This concept means that each individual is allowed the foremost right to have his

Chapter Four

own perspective on his conflict and express it in his own manner.

Lack of validation is the primary reason for conflict's escalation because such lack throws people into a more defensive and adversarial stance ... they become very positional.

KEY POINT

Individuals who are not allowed to "be" in conflict will fight for the right to have their conflict, which ultimately means to have the right to their own perspectives. Thus, one can appreciate that allowing an individual the right to "be" in conflict is one of the very first steps to resolving any conflict.

Again, it is important to realize that validation of a person, his ideas or his position allows the proper and orderly engagement of conflict. Validation needs to occur in each block of the process, but is vital at the early stage of the conflict resolution process. Acknowledgement and engagement of another's position at the early stage can prevent defensiveness and speed up the resolution process. For example, in a divorce situation, acknowledging the husband's position of wanting full custody of the minor children at the beginning of the process (1) does not mean he will ultimately achieve his goal, or (2) does not mean that the wife agrees with him ... she probably wants full custody, too. What it *does* mean is that his hopes and desires as a father are acknowledged when we validate him and say, "So,

Seeing Through The Wall

I hear you want full custody of your minor children. Is that correct?" Of course, his answer is yes, and he recognizes that his position is acknowledged/validated.

For validation to be effective, the individual being validated must sense his right to presently exist as he is, to think how he thinks, and to feel how he feels. Thus, a statement that reflects his present self is vital. For example, one late night at an airport in Texas, when all the flights were delayed, I took the opportunity to validate a counter agent. She appeared seven months pregnant, extremely tired, frustrated with the delays … not to mention the complaints of my fellow passengers. I simply stated the obvious in a verbal reflection of what appeared to be her present state of mind and health. I said with an honest tone of voice, "You appear to be handling the situation very well considering the late night, customer complaints, and you're having to stand so much." She smiled, agreed with me and took my ticket. Later, to my surprise, I was upgraded to first class. I feel the ticket agent "rewarded" me for the validation she received.

In conflict situations, validating the other person's right to be angry or to disagree with you works well. Individuals in conflict are not accustomed to the right of having their own opinion or ideas expressed without counter–argument from the very beginning. Simple phrases such as: "I see you are very angry with me, and I hear that you feel your position is right in this situation," can do wonders. Such a statement literally gives the other person the right to express his anger and opinion without opposition at this initial stage of the conflict resolution process. (Your added opinion will come later in the process when you ADD your opinion for consideration.) Please note: you have not agreed with the expressed anger or opinion. You have only acknowledged both as a fact. Within the validation process, others must sense (from your verbal and non–verbal communication) that you are not attempting to oppose their position or depreciate them as a person. For example, think of someone who opposed you or your attitudes regarding a particular subject. Possibly your spouse is upset because you spend too much money on your clothing and personal care. Acknowledging his anger with the proper words will validate his feelings and his right to have these feelings based upon his present knowledge of the situation or conflict. Of course you will have plenty to say on the subject later; however, for now you are working the process to validate your husband. Thus, proper validation would sound like this: "I hear that you are upset with the amount of money I spend on clothes and personal care. Is that right?" Such a response simply states facts regarding what your spouse felt, almost word for word, and asks the question of whether the response was accurate. This questioning accomplishes two major tasks. First, it shows the fact that you heard your husband. Second, it demonstrates that you want to be correct with your response.

> ## KEY POINT
> Validating statements are verbal and accurate repetitions of:
> - What a person stated
> - The feelings attached to the statements
> - A reflection of the environment surrounding the statement
> - A request for accuracy
>
> Validating statements are made with a non-patronizing and neutral tone of voice.

Validating feelings of hostility or defensiveness prevents the other person from being able to use these emotions in a manipulative manner. We say to the other person, in effect, "You are angry and hostile <u>at this present moment</u> and I acknowledge that fact for now. I am also willing to talk about what specifically made you angry. Fair enough?" Such open acknowledgement effectively takes the air out of the hot air balloon of anger because once the emotion has been openly mentioned, the person hesitates to use it manipulatively again. In conflict, emotions are often used to get attention. Once the attention has been appropriately given through validation, the need for attention goes away because you have properly acknowledged the feeling and attitude of the person.

Validate Early and Often

The validation process can be compared to the emergency room of a hospital. Patients are brought into the hospital in severe medical conflict. Each patient presents many medical issues ... stop the bleeding, open an air passage, determine what caused the injury or sickness, to mention a few. Physicians cannot prescribe a treatment plan until the patient is stable and his full medical condition is known. In other words, the emergency room accepts the patient as he is and in turn validates his present medical condition before other medical decisions are made. Based upon this initial medical validation, other tests or medical issues may then be explored in detail. An operation may be needed immediately. The analogy is the patient is acknowledged in his medical conflict as he currently presents himself to the emergency room doctors. And the physicians, whether they like it or not, can't alter this medical condition without acknowledging it first, and then working with the conditions to change them for the better. Emergency room doctors, nurses, and technicians know how to properly engage medical conflict. They see real life conflict every day of their practice.

If the physicians did not medically validate the patient's present position, disastrous consequences could result. For example, after a serious fall on a hard object then on a hard floor, my ribs felt very painful ... not to mention the pain in my back. This was my second serious fall, and I was already on narcotic pain medication. In the emergency room, the doctor felt I was faking my injury to get other prescription drugs. Thus, the doctor refused to validate my severe pain or verbal statements. Based upon the doctor's reaction, I suffered severely for lack of proper immediate treatment. In truth, the lack of physician validation closed down further discussion of testing or pain relief treatment. Without the physician validating my pain, no further discussions or tests were run since the physician was in charge. I was just left suffering. On the other hand, subsequent demands for test allowed the physician new information upon which to change his mind. By analogy, personal conflict needs to be handled as though the person was presenting to you as a treating physician. The individual's position needs to be perceived without criticism or judgment and properly acknowledged, then discussed and tested for reliability. (I did get a formal letter of apology from the doctor.)

Another analogy from maritime history will also prove the point. When the Titanic was on its maiden voyage, it hit an iceberg in the Atlantic Ocean. Although this "unsinkable" luxury liner was indeed sinking, the power structure on board (the builder, the captain, etc.) refused to validate the actual condition of their liner until it was too late and lives were lost due to panic. Had the actual condition of this life threatening disaster been acknowledged earlier, possibly lives could have been saved by a more orderly emergency procedure. One can only imagine the escalation of conflict that evening on board the Titanic.

Chapter Four

Hopefully, most conflicts will not be as life threatening as the Titanic tragedy. Nevertheless, these analogies speak to the essential need for early and proper validation of conflict, whether or not the position of the presenting party is correct or not.

It is important to validate the other person at the start of a conflict, otherwise, the other individual may feel it necessary to defend his position throughout the process. People cannot concentrate on hearing and digesting new information when they are spending their energy defending themselves, their existing ideas, or their position. People in conflict are so accustomed to pushing hard to be really heard, they expect to fight for their position or point of view. Until they feel heard and understood, the pushing and fighting will continue. They can't listen to anyone else's ideas because all their energy is spent advancing their own position.

By validating individuals and their thinking at the beginning of a conflict, others will not have to spend time and energy defending themselves from a perceived fear of change or other subconscious fear. From past experiences in conflict, individuals fear having to change their thinking or behavior. Change is difficult for individuals, therefore, it will be fought at all cost.

The perceived fear of change due to divorce is very real for a wife and mother. Consciously, she knows some day soon she will be a single mom. Subconsciously, she knows new and scary relationships lay ahead since she has never been a single mom. By validating this fear of the future at the start of the divorce process, she will be allowed the right to have this fear and not have to subconsciously deal with it in the negotiations for divorce. The fear becomes a factor or issue that is now out on the table. Her fear becomes recognized and acknowledged as having a bearing on how she perceives the settlement terms presented to her. Having this fear validated helps both sides in the negotiations because fear of the future (or uncertainty) is a major factor which limits settlement in divorce or conflict in general.

KEY POINT

Validation needs to take place as early as possible in the process to prevent the other person from having to press his position over and over again until he feels you have heard him.

Until each party validates the initial position of the other, both parties will restate their ideas or beliefs for as long as it takes to get recognition from the other party. Because most people have not been properly trained to engage conflict, they assume that their position, ideas, or thinking will be challenged … especially since the term "yes, but" is employed so often in conflict.

Amazingly, proper validation will tear down the veil of defensive behavior. Once the individual perceives that he will not have to forcefully defend his present position,

Chapter Four

true communication can begin in earnest. After a person is validated, his verbal and non-verbal communication changes, like letting the air out of a tight balloon – slowly the balloon gets smaller and looks less taut. The harshness in the eyes soften, the shoulders relax, as do the arms. The defensive tension flows out of the person. Not only does his body relax, but his words soften to a more reasonable tone and become more logical.

In one of my divorce mediations, the husband got mad and threw a large chair across the conference room. Shortly thereafter, I separated the parties into two conference rooms. As the mediator, I validated the husband's anger and frustration at his wife by asking, "How does your wife push your buttons to make you mad?" He then proceeded to vent and let the hot air of anger out of his system. Because his anger was validated without humiliation, he became much less defensive of his position during the mediation. I basically said to him, through validation, "I get that your wife, this divorce situation, and this mediation are making you very angry. Can we talk about it?" Realistically, he feared what might happen based upon past conflict with his wife. She would push his buttons and he would get angry and throw things, thus loosing credibility. By validating the root of his problem, the fear of communicating with his wife, we could then begin logical discussions. He was no longer defensive and was willing to proceed with the divorce mediation without fear.

Once this transformation happens, people can begin to hear and process new information. A dialogue can now begin on the issues at hand. Energy can be devoted to discussions of the main points of each issue; there is no need to defend against a fear of loss or failure of one's position to be acknowledged by the other party. You can see the people relax or stop other defensive non-verbal communication *after proper validation* because they realize they do not have to fight for the right to be themselves or defend their present position. Proper validation allows the people to be and think as they are now ... warts and all.

Steps to Validation

Validation is easy to accomplish. The steps in the validation process are as follows:

Smile

Be mentally aware that the other individual may be on the defensive and use a smile to signal cooperation. A proper smile is like a firm handshake. It is engaging but not threatening. A smile signals cooperation and friendliness in any language, and is a powerful non-verbal tool of peace. On the other hand, a fake smile or grin will be interpreted as superiority or glibness. Be real and honest with your smile so it is interpreted properly. In my experience when I smile at a person, they usually smile back at me. Nothing is said, yet there is a feeling of

Chapter Four

reciprocity. This feeling is beneficial for the validation process.

Keep an Appropriate Space

Do not get too close to the other person with your body, since being too close may cause the other person to think you're trying to overpower her. Keeping an appropriate distance at the start of conflict is essential so the other person feels safe and secure. Set boundaries for yourself by keeping at least an arm's length away so the other person will not feel like he has to move away and disengage for his own safety. Distance also sends a non-verbal message that you are not a threat. In addition, it shows respect for the space of the other person and becomes validating in and of itself as a non-verbal gesture of peaceful coexistence.

Be a Mirror Image

Try to be a mirror image of the other person's body posture without being obvious. When people see themselves in others, they like what they see. If someone is standing with hands on their hips and you subtly put your hands on your hips, it would appear that both of you were looking at a mirror image of the other. This mirror image or reflection in body positions signals a similarity or congruity of two people in their stance. Such a congruity promotes an attitude of cooperation as opposed to opposition. If the body positions are not a mirror image of each other, it signals a difference in stance and possibly opposition. For example, one person is standing with his hands on his hips, yet the other person has folded her arms around her chest. One person is open and non–protected by their posture, while the other has arms defensively folded in a protective stance. Such differences in body position creates non–verbal communication that shouts different feelings at the moment of contact.

Even if the defensive looking body stance is caused by the person being cold, it is better to match it, as this non–verbally validates the other's feelings at the time. In my experience, once the body position is matched, the other person relaxes and moves their hands away from a defensive posture to a less defensive one.

A Non–Judgmental and Affirming Response

Attempt to repeat what the individual is communicating to you without adding any verbal or non–verbal judgment or criticism. The exact words a person uses are very important to that person or he would not use them. Beginners tend to be embarrassed by repeating the exact words of the other person because they think they will sound like a parrot. Therefore, out of embarrassment they use too many of their own words and jeopardize the validation process. Any attempt to change the words to what you think they mean is an attempt to second–guess the speaker. Changing the words to what you think they mean is like adding a judgment as to what the other person stated. "That is not what I said or meant," is usually their response before things escalate creating further argument. To repeat their words exactly is to honor other people. Being precise in your words declares to the person, "I have listened so well to you that I can repeat exactly what you said", or, "I got exactly what you said." Keep in mind the old saying, that "imitation is the most sincere form of flattery." Repeating the key words and phrases is extremely flattering to the other person and says that you cared enough to listen, hear, and know exactly what the other person said. This communication technique is very rare today because people tend not to listen to others well enough to repeat exactly what was said, or may listen with their own judgment interfering with what they heard.

A Neutral Tonality

Validating statements are most effective using a neutral, non-patronizing tone of voice. This technique allows the other person's exact words to be repeated without sounding false or fake. Use the phrasing, "What I heard you say was," then repeat exactly what you heard them say, followed by, "Is that right?" This method has several benefits. First, if you do a good job, the other person has to acknowledge to himself that you did listen well and did "get" exactly what he said. Second, no fight or disagreement arises because you did not change the speaker's words or their meaning. Third, the only response to your question in most instances is "yes." If the response is "no", simply ask, "What part did I miss?"

The other person then feels obligated to tell you. When he tells you what you missed, simply repeat the response and ask if your new response is correct. Either way, what was actually stated will be validated.

Utilize Listening Skills

When people talk, listen completely.
Most people never listen.
Ernest Hemingway

True validation takes effort, time, and a little practice. Many of us need to hone our listening skills so that we can fully hear everything the other person is telling us without worrying about how we are going to respond. There is no need for a defensive response when we validate. That is one beauty of validation. We only repeat the substance of what the other person said, using their own words. So don't worry about your position or answer at the time of validation. Just listen and capture what the other person wants you to hear without any judgment on your part.

Chapter Four

> **KEY POINT**
>
> Remember – validation is not agreement! Validation is a communication process, not an end result. Validation of the person, her ideas and concepts helps to move the discussion process forward because it lowers the defensiveness of both parties. When we validate we do not agree fully; however, we give immediate recognition to the other person's perspective on a conflict issue.

THE TIMING OF VALIDATION

Remember, the most current position or idea of the other person is the only idea or position being validated at the early stage of the V.A.L.U.E. System. Validation is only step one of the process. Validation is necessary to acknowledge all parties and positions as they are, <u>before</u> further discussions take place. It is like saying, "I will listen to your side if you will listen to mine without judging me in advance. Please let me explain my thinking and feelings." Extending this idea of acknowledging new ideas or issues, Validation will occur at <u>every</u> point where new information is presented.

> **KEY POINT**
>
> **CONTINUALLY VALIDATE**
>
> Validation changes the dynamics of the dispute process and opens up communication. Although validation is the first block in the V.A.L.U.E. System, it needs to be used throughout the dispute process when there is a need to acknowledge a new idea, position, concept, feeling or person.

I always attempt to validate most people and their ideas. Validation is a wonderful communication technique for every-day use because it lets the other person know you are listening and honoring him as a person.

Improper Validation

Improper validation occurs when (1) a sugary or patronizing tone of voice is employed, (2) our words or meanings are substituted for those of the other person or (3) we don't get agreement that our response is acceptable or complete enough to capture the true meaning of the speaker's communication. You will know instantly if validation has failed. The other party will still look, act, or talk defensively. At this point wisely check the three points mentioned above and try again. Try changing your tonality to a more neutral tone. Check

Chapter Four

your communication to make sure a judgmental phrase did not slip into your response.

If the situation is still the same, then another approach is necessary. Be direct and say: "I sense that I have missed what you want me to hear. Please tell me what that is." Many times people play games and try to block your proper validation. However, this statement is so sincere it usually stops the game playing. Next, you will hear the real message. This statement may be very similar to others you have heard, but game is over. Simply validate the new statement.

Validation Sets the Agenda

When validation occurs, a person, idea, position, definition, perception, concept or other fact is acknowledged and allowed to be placed in dialogue without judgment or change. What this step produces is initial information about one side of a conflict. Normally, at the start, one validates the other person and his original position in the conflict. The validation basically sets an agenda for later discussions. For example, if spouses were arguing over finances, the wife may set up an agenda of her husband's position and his beliefs on the subject. The agenda of issues to talk about would look like the following:

Husband's Position: Wife spends too much money on clothes and personal items.

Husband's Beliefs:

a) Too many of the same color shoes
b) Too many face powders and shades of lipsticks
c) Too many "church" dresses

Verbally, the process would sound like this:

Validate the Husband's Position:

"Husband, I hear you telling me that I spend too much money on clothes and personal items."

Validate Husband's Beliefs:

"Specifically you talk about three main categories. One: shoes; two: make–up items; and three: too many 'church' clothes." "Is that Correct?" Since the former factual statements were exactly what her husband said, the only correct answer is "yes."

We have now set the agenda for discussion through the validation process. In listing form it looks like this:

Chapter Four

Conflict / Discussion Agenda	
Husband	**Wife**
<u>Position:</u> Wife spends too much money on clothes and personal items.	<u>Position:</u> Money spent on personal items is appropriate.
<u>Beliefs:</u>	<u>Beliefs:</u>
1. Too many of the same color shoes	… will come later in the next chapter – *keep reading!*
2. Too many face powders and shades of lipsticks	
3. Too many "church" dresses	

It is important to validate the individual and his position before you go to the next step of adding any information about your position or concepts relating to the conflict. All parties are free to change their ideas and positions in the future, based upon new information they obtain within the upcoming talks and discussions. During the other stages of the V.A.L.U.E. process, parties add new information about positions, and now learning will take place between the parties. Once the position is fully explored in all of its parts and meanings, a new understanding will emerge between the parties that will allow either person the freedom to change his position. I often hear, "Well, knowing that new information, I am willing to discuss a new way to handle custody of the children."

THE V.A.L.U.E. SYSTEM GUIDE

Concept	Definition	When to Use	Words to Use
VALIDATE	A communication technique which assures another person they have been fully heard, and acknowledged. The communication acknowledges them as a person, and also their ideas. Validation does not equal agreement with the other person or his ideas. Validation acknowledges a *right* to be a unique person and express your own ideas.	At every opportunity to confirm and acknowledge the other person or his perspective. Validation is used throughout every block of the system.	"I hear you say (then repeat what they said as closely to their exact words as possible). Then ask: "Is that correct?" or "Did I get that right?" If I didn't get it right, I ask, "What is right?" When they respond, repeat what they said and affirm your restatement as correct.

Chapter Five

*Remember: No one can make you feel
inferior without your consent.*
Eleanor Roosevelt

V.A.L.U.E. BLOCK TWO: ADD YOUR PERSPECTIVE

Add Your Perspective

Once the person, his position, beliefs or issues have been properly validated (as seen in Chapter IV) an agenda of issues can be set up for dialogue. For this dialogue your own supplementary information needs to be placed on the agenda. Now is the time to ADD your beliefs and issues.. This addition is an easy process of using a simple phrase like, "Now that I have heard your beliefs/issues, I need to ADD my beliefs/issues." Then add your beliefs. For example, let's continue with the husband and wife discussion from Chapter IV.

Our spouses' conflict/discussion would look like this agenda after the wife finished adding her three beliefs.

Conflict / Discussion Agenda	
Husband	Wife
Position: Wife spends too much money on clothes and personal items.	Position: Money spent on personal items is appropriate.
Beliefs or Issues:	Beliefs or Issues:
1. Too many of the same color shoes	1. Need shoes for work
2. Too many face powders and shades of lipsticks	2. Stay in style
3. Too many "church" dresses	3. Need to look good socially

From the information disclosed above, the wife added her beliefs that the money spent on personal items for her was necessary (her position) because of the issues of 1) work, 2) style, and 3) looking good socially. She was able to add this information to the agenda for discussion because she did not discount her husband's views. She validated them and added hers instead of using a "yes, but" technique.

In replying to the confrontation of others, many people make the mistake of using the phrase "yes, but", "yes, however", or a variation of this phrase. The phrase, "I understand/hear what you are saying, *but*" is a commonly used phrase in conflictive conversations. Using the word "*but*" puts the other person on the defensive by discounting what was previously stated or expressed.

Chapter Five

What is heard by the other individual is, "I only listened to you to be nice, because my ideas are much better than yours," or, "I don't care what you say, my thoughts on this subject control." The result of the "yes, but" phrasing destroys the previous validation and throws both parties back on the defensive. At this point, each party has to fight harder to get his issues acknowledged and a vicious cycle of polarization begins. Each person attempts to gain power over the other person with facts and information to prove his point or ideology. Such communication throws the parties into a boxing ring. One person wins when the other is knocked out or throws in the towel and quits. When this happens, the parties are worse off than before because each party is stuck in their original position and dialogue ceases.

In many "yes, but" situations, we are dealing with individual perceptions which become reality. One person perceives a conflict with his chosen "facts", while the other person perceives the same conflict with her set of "facts." The incident, idea, or circumstance exists with two different set of "facts." For example in an automobile accident several witnesses can report seeing different causes of the accident. In a sporting event, referees can call a play differently depending upon their position on the field. Each witness or referee feels he is correct from his perspective. The point is that we need to recognize this phenomenon and validate it by the proper phrases of "addition", not words that devalue another. Each party has the right to add anything to the discussion and have it validated. This addition of information does not mean that the other party must accept the statement as true

Seeing Through The Wall

or genuine ... only that each party has the right to state their own version of the facts as they currently know them to be.

By using the "add" technique, each person can feel validated in what he is attempting to express. At a minimum, each person is heard and not discounted by the other individual. This addition of information can be viewed by the other party as new information and not as a discount of his perception. This concept is important to the building blocks of conflict resolution. We resolve conflict differences based upon our hearing and processing of information we did not know before the conflict dialogue. By allowing an 'addition' process where new information can emerge, the parties are building a reserve of new information that will later be clarified and acted upon in the Learn and Understand blocks. Resolution cannot be achieved based upon the rehash of old information or information which is not interpreted as valid. In conflict resolution terms, new information can emerge after validating and acknowledging the "old or heard before" information of each party. Otherwise, the parties are not ready to receive new information because they are pushing the other party to validate the old information. Once acknowledged each party can add his new information to the existing and validated information. Also due to this process, parties in conflict may begin to hear, see, and feel information for the first time as "new" information, even if the information was "old" or "heard before".

Adding your perspective, beliefs, or issues may appear simple; however, you need to keep a few techniques in mind. Following these pointers will enable a smooth addition process.

Chapter Five

> **KEY POINT**
>
> By using the "add" technique, each person can feel validated in what he is attempting to express. At a minimum, each person is heard and not discounted by the other individual. This addition of information can be viewed by the other party as new information and not as a discount of his perception. This concept is important to the building blocks of conflict resolution.

ORGANIZE YOUR PERSPECTIVE/POSITION

Analyze your thoughts and perspective into beliefs that give support to your position. As in an English class, thinking about our theme and its parts in a logical manner is extremely helpful to communication. Instead of a stream of sentences flowing into a river of thoughts, we need to think of our main theme or position as a structure supported by three columns or a circle with three main sections as in Diagram VIII.

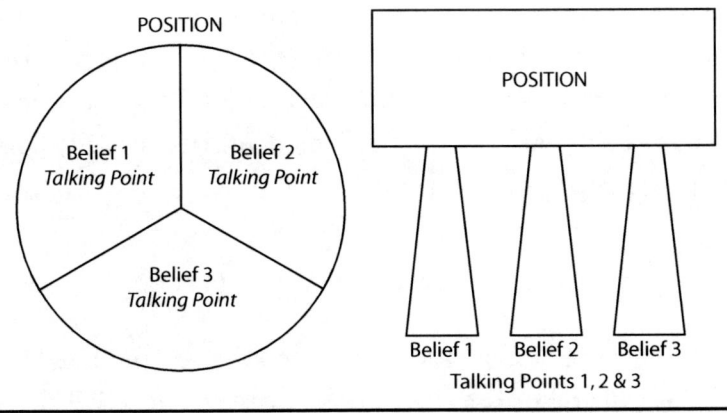

Diagram VIII – Organization of Perspective / Position

Seeing Through The Wall

Our three beliefs, or talking points, support our position on any particular subject. They are what we ADD as our perspective to the dialogue with the other party. Like English class, where we were asked to support our theme. These three points are the substance of each person's conflict theme. It is important to outline and validate these points, taken from each side, so that everyone is clear as to the meaning of the position in controversy. If parties don't take time to clearly spell out meanings, each side may be just guessing or assuming what the other person believes. One makes assumptions based upon old information from a previous encounter on the subject. Let's take the concept of "savings" for an example. Without one's beliefs being explained, "savings" could mean money left to spend as opposed to money put aside for a rainy day.

Furthermore, asking for and organizing beliefs into a logical structure makes each party think clearly about the beliefs which support her position. When these beliefs are validated as talking points in a dialogue (see Chapter IV) and restated clearly to the speaker, she may really hear them for the first time as statements of fact. Thus, she may not like what these statements express ... and she is then entitled to change her statements to better reflect her position or beliefs. Such a change will further clarify the dialogue because she is communicating new information. In Chapter VI, you will see this concept demonstrated.

Keep Issues to Three

Structure your "agenda" into three (or less) major beliefs or talking points from your perspective with the most current information you have available.

Chapter Five

Communication works best if there are only three major beliefs in support of your position. Preachers are often trained to have three major points in their sermons since people often have trouble grasping or discussing too many issues at one time. Limiting your conversations to three main points in a conflict situation is generally the most workable and ultimately successful.

Keep in mind you are listing your perspective, talking points or beliefs according to the most current information you know on this subject. You are adding information that is hopefully new to the other party. Such information may not have been disclosed before or it may be very recent. By example, you may have previously discussed a problem with your boss to no avail. Perhaps there is new information you have to support your position. Presenting this new information in a logical manner would be most appropriate for discussion in comparison to the information discussed before. Even if there is no new or different information, you still need to outline in three points your beliefs so they are put on the table for dialogue.

USE SIMPLE WORDS AND PHRASES

Express your issues in a few simple words or a phrase. Beliefs, issues or talking points need to be expressed in as few descriptive words as possible. Long sentences are difficult for people to process, and a phrase needs to be seven words or less. Simple words and phrases are digestible by the other party and less intimidating to them. Most people find using simple words and phrases difficult because they often get nervousness and ramble. Remember, this phrase is the start of the dialogue. As the V.A.L.U.E. system progresses, you will have more time to further define and clarify the fine points of your perspectives on these talking points. For now, use the KISS Method of Keep It Simple and Short.

In divorce mediation, I hear general terms like trust, unfaithful, honesty, running around or love. These words are the beliefs that support the position of "I want a divorce." They look like this:

POSITION
"I WANT A DIVORCE"

- Unfaithful
- No Love
- No Trust

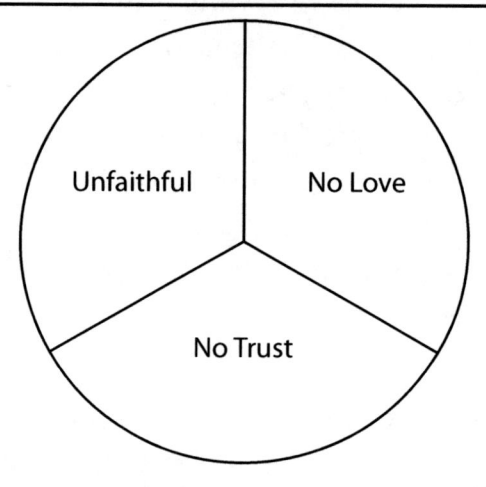

Diagram IX – Beliefs Supporting Position of "I want a divorce"

At this early stage, these are the general reasons one spouse wants a divorce. While they are too broad for any final resolutions, they are fine for this stage of the process. We can obtain their true meanings in this

Chapter Five

divorce case through the Learning process or the next block of the V.A.L.U.E. system. These broad concepts are all we need now.

Your Beliefs Can Be Different

Your beliefs or issues don't have to be the same as the other person's. Often in conflict, each party will have different reasons for his position. This circumstance is absolutely fine. Truly exploring their differences later on in the V.A.L.U.E. process is necessary for resolutions, and is what happens in the "Learn and Understand" blocks. For now, some beliefs, issues, or talking points can be the same and some can be different. The important point is to put positions and beliefs side by side for each party to observe and discuss. In a divorce case, the positions and beliefs might look like those in Diagram X:

DIFFERENT BELIEFS IN A DIVORCE CONFLICT

HUSBAND'S POSITION NO DIVORCE	WIFE'S POSITION DIVORCE
The affair is over / Love for Her / No Trust	He is unfaithful / No love for Him / No Trust

Diagram X – Different Beliefs in a Divorce Conflict

As can be seen from Diagram X, the positions are total opposites and so are some issues. Clearly, each party (for personal reasons) has "no trust" for the other. These issues will be further defined later in the 'Learn and Understand' blocks of this system, but for now we have all we need to move forward to the Learn block.

Be Non–Threatening and Factual

Express your beliefs in a non–threatening and factual way to the other party. To prevent defensive behavior that might destroy your validation in Block I, express your beliefs as simple facts at this stage with a neutral tone of voice. You don't need to fully explain each reason at this time. In a divorce, a simple, "I don't love him anymore," is more appropriate as a factual conclusion than, "For years I have had a problem staying in love with him because he has changed so much since we got married seven years ago." This last statement has too many aspects of disagreement to bring forth at this time. These aspects may come up later, but for now use the KISS method and keep it simple and short.

Use "I" Based Statements

In adding your beliefs or talking points, use "I" based statements. Statements that begin with "I" do not cast blame on the other person because they don't contain an "I am blaming you" aspect in the discussions. For example, "I don't love you anymore," places the reason

Chapter Five

for non—love solely on the speaker. This is vastly different from, "You made me stop loving you." The last statement states the same conclusion but with an "I am blaming you" attitude from the start. This wording places the responsibility squarely on the other person. We may feel the other person is responsible for our conflict; however, we must state our beliefs as our own, and as though we are solely responsible for the content. Therefore, we use "I" based statements. An "I" followed by a feeling, thought, or perspective communicates sole ownership of the meaning. One may disagree with "I" based statements, but such a style of communication does not cast blame or ridicule on the one who disagrees. Hardly anything for the party who disagrees to be defensive remains because the speaker took all the responsibility for the belief or action. "I don't trust my husband," places all the actions and responsibility on the wife and adequately expresses her belief as a fact for later discussion.

Sandy, a mediator friend, claims that using "I" based statements is critical to conflict resolution. She wishes more people would employ "I" based statements in their regular conversations at home, socially, and at work. Using these statements, she claims, virtually eliminates defensiveness by the person receiving the communication. With the proper tonality, an "I" based statement can establish a boundary line by the speaker; thereby, creating a neutral zone in the conflict. "I" based statement don't infringe on the territory of an opponent. They only express the territorial responsibility of the speaker. Thus, they show respect for the other person. Some readers may have been taught that the use of "I" statements is selfish. In conflict resolution however, the "I" statement is necessary to indicate ownership of a statement without placing blame.

USE "NEED" BASED STATEMENTS

Also, it is important to express your beliefs in need–based statements instead of want–based statements. People don't always get what they want in life because the 'want' appears to be discretionary. However, others are more likely to give people what they 'need'. That's just human nature. For example, people will permit you to butt in line only if they perceive you have a compelling need (the door is about to be shut on my airplane) as opposed to just wanting to advance your position in the line. Therefore, add your beliefs in a "need" based statement and there is a greater chance you will be validated. Use the simple phrase, "I need to add my issues to what you said. They are Issue 1, Issue 2, and Issue 3" is adequate. This phrasing puts your beliefs or issues on the table alongside the other person's talking points. Now you have effectively added your issues, beliefs, or perspective to the conflict negotiation.

Chapter Five

> **KEY POINT**
>
> The use of "I" based statements allows you to own your idea and not blame the other person. Also, the use of a "need" based statement allows the other person to see how important your perception or belief is to you. In combination, an "I" and "need" based statement express ownership rights in a belief without blaming the other person.

Hidden Agendas

Many times some part of a communication is left out or hidden on purpose so the full story can't be known. When there are hardly any additions to the communications, there may be hidden agendas or issues. When you ask if there is anything more to add and the other person doesn't fully answer you or becomes defensive, there is probably a hidden agenda. If this defensive communication happens, be sure their old information has been validated. Next ask if there is anything else they would like to tell you and use the process again. More often than not, the missing information will be expressed because you sensed that something was missing and asked. Then simply validate the new information and go on.

The Effect of Adding Your Perspective, Idea or Belief

The Harvard Negotiation Project is most credited with the concept of the "and" stance. They state that the act of understanding what someone says doesn't require you to forfeit your own belief. Regardless of the strength of each perception or belief, both parties matter. In conflict it does not have to be "my way or the highway" thinking. My grandmother used to say to me, "There are three sides to an argument. They are your side, my side, and the right side." She understood the "and" concept. Not surprisingly, she had many friends and few enemies. The "and" concept validates both sides of the conflict and sets the stage for dialogue in the 'Learn and Understand' blocks of this system. The "and" concept sets the agenda for the logical discussion of the issues on both sides. It allows the parties to see the similarities and differences in both side's positions. This 'Add' block sets up a more even playing field for the conflict because both side's positions and issues are exposed.

THE V.A.L.U.E. SYSTEM GUIDE

Concept	Definition	When to Use	Words to Use
ADD	A communication strategy to validate the other person's perspectives or belief's, then to ADD your own perceptions, values, beliefs, attitudes or ideas.	Every time you need to ADD your perspective to any discussion or dialogue.	"I hear you are saying (Repeat the perspective), and I would like to ADD my perspective. My perspective is [then state your perspective]. CAVEAT: Never use the "yes, but" expression as the language discounts what the other person presented. The expression implies "yes, but my ideas are better."

Chapter Six

We shall not cease from exploration and the end of all our exploring will be to arrive where we started and know the place for the first time.
T. S. Elliot

A mind that is stretched by a new experience can never go back to its old dimensions.
Oliver Wendell Holmes

V.A.L.U.E. BLOCK THREE: HOW TO LEARN

LEARN

The Validation and Add processes have set an agenda for discussion, and now it is time for the full dialogue of each issue or belief. The Learn process can flow naturally due to the validation of each person's positions and issues or beliefs. During this stage parties begin to hear, see, and feel the substance of the issues contained in both their positions. Parties begin to learn the parts and pieces of each issue. They learn the perspectives, values, facts, beliefs or assumptions underlying the other party's issues which were not evident before this block. Hopefully, such information becomes "new information" to each party. With this new in depth information, each party is able to form a different perspective of the conflict. This new perspective can be transformed into a new concept for negotiation. Through the Learn dialogue, we re-cycle and transform the substance of old issues into new concepts for dialogue and later negotiation in the Understand block. This educational process must happen before people try to "understand" each other through discussions of differences in concepts, values, beliefs, or other conflicting issues. Without this continuous educational process, there is little new knowledge for negotiations. New knowledge is now available for future discussions and resolution.

Power Imbalances

Power imbalances may exist between the parties. Power imbalances of money, authority, position, etc., can inhibit resolution. Without a learning block to obtain new information, parties in a power position to decide outcomes operate from old knowledge or their old perception of a policy, event, or conflict. Thus, the conflict dialogue contains nothing new for discussion and negotiation.

The following power and knowledge paradigm shows that those with power to decide (upper left hand corner) need to be educated by those with the greatest awareness (lowest right hand corner) (and often the lowest power) in order to resolve power imbalances and continue the dialogue toward negotiation. Providing Learning (upper right hand corner) pulls the party in power into this right hand corner.

Chapter Six

This party now possesses both the power and complete awareness to address the needs of people in this situation.

```
POWER TO DECIDE
100% │ Needs Education
     │ A person with Great   │ Learning Needed to
     │ Power and Little      │ Pull Knowledge up
     │ Knowledge or Care     │ to a Higher Power
     │                       │ Position
     │              Moves Over →
     │                ↖ Education
     │ A person with Little  │ A person with Great
     │ Knowledge and         │ Knowledge but
     │ Lower Power           │ Lower Power
     │                       │
     │                       │ Provides Education
  0% └───────────────────────┴──────────────────
     0%                    50%              100%
              FULL KNOWLEDGE ABOUT ISSUES
```

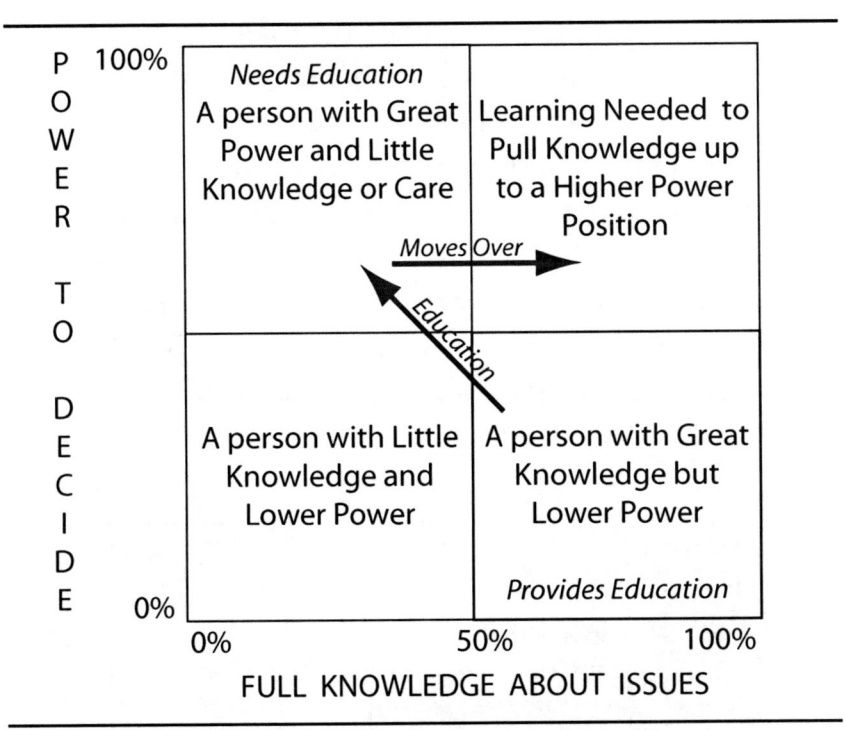

Diagram XI – Power & Knowledge Paradigm

Power imbalances occur in most conflict. Rarely is there an even playing field. Conflict escalates where there is a dispute between a party with great power to make decisions and another party with less power, but with a great awareness of a problem. The best example of this situation is the strife during the civil rights movement in The United States of America in the nineteen–sixties and seventies. The controlling parties in the United States legislatures had little awareness or compassion for the problems of the black communities. The Civil Rights Movement created an awareness of black issues needing to be addressed. As a result, the United States Supreme Court and the United States legislatures changed laws affecting black equality.

The same principle applies to power imbalances in personal or business conflict. In the following diagram XII, the boss (through his position of authority) has more power than the employee. Both are in conflict because the employee has first hand knowledge and awareness about a production problem at work. The boss will still make business decisions from a position of high power and low knowledge. Until the employee is able to present this knowledge to his boss, there will be nothing new to discuss to change the position of the boss, and conflict will continue.

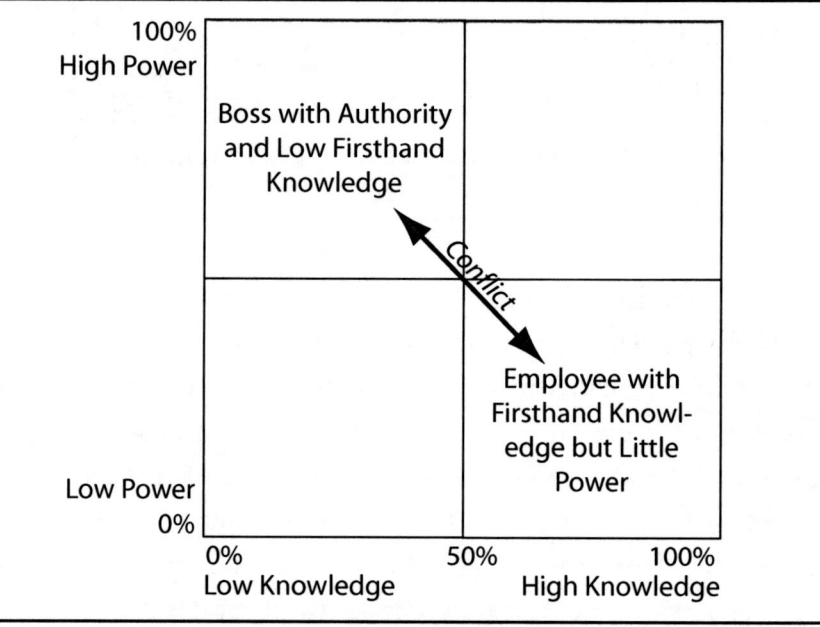

Diagram XII – Power & Knowledge Imbalance Conflict

Chapter Six

In Diagram XIII, the employee must educate the boss about the production problems so the boss will move into a position of high power and high knowledge. Once the employee properly engages the conflict and follows a process to educate the boss, new information is presented that enables the boss to learn about the work problems. This Learn process puts both parties on a more even playing field for future dialogue and negotiation. The result is the employee feels validated and the boss can now make an educated decision about the production problem while maintaining her power position of power. In one situation I dealt with, a boss did not understand the need for more office space. The employee's department was working out of a kitchen in order to have enough room to operate. Once the boss actually toured the departmental space he ordered new space.

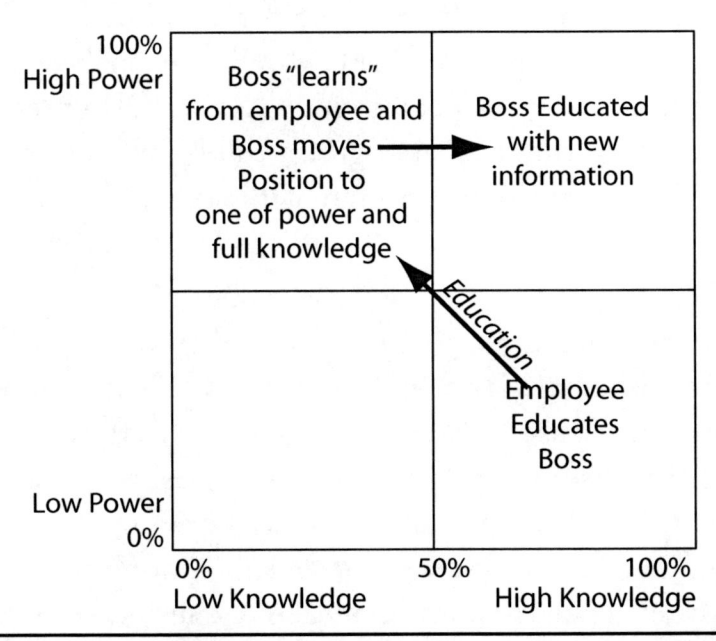

```
100%
High Power | Boss "learns"       |
           | from employee and    | Boss Educated
           | Boss moves  ──────▶  | with new
           | Position to          | information
           | one of power and     |
           | full knowledge       |
           |                      ╲Education
           |                       ╲
           |                      Employee
           |                      Educates
           |                      Boss
Low Power
0%
           0%                    50%              100%
           Low Knowledge                  High Knowledge
```

Diagram XIII – Resolving Power & Knowledge Imbalance Conflict

Transforming and Recycling Issues

The Learn block is a transformation phase. The Learn block allows us to move from the positions to the substance of the issues. Thus, we effectively eliminate the original position from further discussion. The original positions have been effectively re–cycled or re–framed into issues for discussion. We will now open each issue as we would a small box of valentine candy. These boxes usually contain three different chocolates. When we open the heart box we can see, feel, and smell the real chocolates. By analogy, when we open up the issues we can see the pieces of new information just like we saw the pieces of chocolate.

In order to disclose the various parts of the issues each party must think, maybe for the first time, about their real substance. Having to describe the parts and pieces of the underlying issues makes people think and analyze their conflict from a deeper perspective. Analysis also prevents discriminatory thinking and "group think" where a group of people just accept a position without true, individual analysis.

When asked to fully explain three reasons for each issue, some people get embarrassed. They have not fully thought through their issues in such detail. This incomplete thinking may cause resistance on their part to fully explain their three reasons for their position. If resistance occurs, validate this resistance to overcome it. For example, use an "I based" statement like, "I sense some hesitation to discuss these issues. I need to know more about your issue or issues. Will you tell me the parts and pieces that make up your issues so I can be clear about what it means?" Or if you feel you know some information that is not disclosed you might say, "I sense that (name the reason(s)) is part of this issue. Is that correct?" And if the other party says "No", then just say, "Will you please tell me which part is correct?" Either way the correct information comes out and is put on the table for discussion and negotiation.

Transform New Knowledge Into Concepts

Also during the Learn block we attempt to transform the information gained by the parts and pieces of the issues into a new concept stated in less than seven words. Forming new information into concepts is not difficult. Let's take a simple example. Suppose someone said to you that an object was red, round, and had a green stem. Your mind would automatically begin to analyze and reason to form a mental picture of several objects. Your mind may see a tomato, an apple, a rose, or other object that fits this general description. Your mind conceptualizes by forming one to three word descriptions of people or events automatically. We classify people as friends, acquaintances, enemies, or bums, based upon our knowledge or perception of the other person. The point here is that we need to actively conceptualize the information we gain from the in–depth discussion of issues into as many short concepts as possible. For example, lack of trust, disloyalty, fairness, or unfaithfulness are examples of new concepts formed through discussion of the issues.

Conceptualizing the information discussed in each issue in a few words demonstrates you have heard and thought enough about the communication to form it into a concept. After you understand the parts and pieces of an issue, you need to simplify the information into a concept that will forward the discussion. You could say, "What you said sounds like the concept of 'lack−of−trust.' Is that correct?" If this sounds correct to the other person, such a statement is very flattering because it proves your sincere desire to really see, hear, and feel what they need to communicate to you.

However if he claims your idea of the concept was wrong then all you have to say is, "Then, please explain the right concept." Usually this produces a statement such as, "What I meant to say was my wife is disloyal to me." Either way, right or corrected, the communication is accurate and confirmed by the other person; therefore, validate the concept as correct. This correct concept can now be discussed without fear of being inaccurate.

Let's take two examples of an employer to employee dispute. The employee defines his position as "disrespect for his employer." The employee has three issues to support his position: 1) unreliable, 2) unfair, and 3) disloyal. These three issues, after dialogue could be lumped together and conceptualized in a phase as, "lack of trust." Once we dialogue and learn about the issues, we are able to form a general new concept. This new concept allows us to re−cycle the key conflict as a "lack of trust" in the employer. The disrespect (the original position) really

Chapter Six

came from a "lack of trust" in the employer based upon the employer's actions. Alternatively another employee, after dialogue, could conceptualize the same three issues as a "bad pay policy" that is 1) unreliably administered, 2) unfair to hourly employees, and 3) disloyal to old timers. In each situation the newly formed concept depends upon the dialogue. We must learn enough to form a concept based upon the dialogue. This conceptualized technique simplifies future discussions because it recycles and reframes the conflict based upon the underlying issues, as opposed to the original surface positions and issues. The following diagram shows a visual representation of the process, as well as an outline of the two examples as a second illustration of how new information is re-cycled or conceptualized.

TRANSFORMING INFORMATION

POSITION

Issue A	Issue B	Issue C

1. New Information
2. New Information
3. New Information

Re-cycle Bin

New Concept
Of Conflict Differences
(from re-cycled Information)

POSITION
Disrespect for Boss

Issue Unreliable	Issue Unfair	Issue Disloyal

New Information
About
Issues

New Concepts
Of Conflict Differences:
"Lack of Trust"
Or
"Bad Pay Policy"

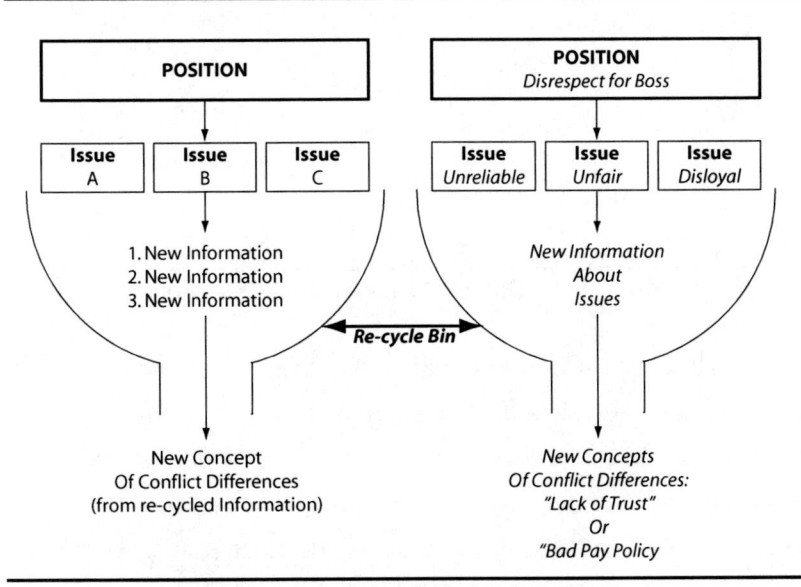

Diagram XIV – Transforming Information

Seeing Through The Wall

> **KEY POINT**
>
> Learning is a full exploration of the substance of each person's issues involved in a conflict. This newly learned information shows the person's meaning behind his issues and can be conceptualized in a few words.

As in Chapter V the positions and issues of a divorcing couple are displayed again in Diagram XV below.

DIFFERENT BELIEFS IN DIVORCE CONFLICT

HUSBAND'S POSITION	WIFE'S POSITION
NO DIVORCE	DIVORCE
The affair is over / Love for Her / No Trust	He is unfaithful / No love for Him / No Trust

Diagram XV – Different Beliefs in Divorce Conflict

Through Validation and Adding, each party is able to outline their basic position and main issues in this hypothetical divorce. During the Learn block we take each party's issues and break them apart to learn the reasons why these issues exist in the first place. It is best to pick one issue at a time for both parties to discuss. Let's

Chapter Six

assume the couple chooses the common issue of "no trust" for exploration. Each party gets to state three reasons for "no trust." The three reasons are shown below.

"No Trust" Issue

HUSBAND'S POSITION NO DIVORCE	WIFE'S POSITION DIVORCE
Lies to Me / Home Life Uncomfortable / Argues with Me	Had an Affair / Stays at Office / Doesn't Talk Anymore

Diagram XVI – "No Trust" Issue

Through discussion both husband and wife declare their perception of the "NO TRUST" issue. From this dialogue we can see the real reasons for mistrusting each other. Also from this new information we can presume that the wife feels abandoned by her husband. He stays away, doesn't talk when he comes home, and even has an affair. Furthermore, we can presume that the husband hates to come home and communicate with his wife… a communication problem at home. He claims she argues with him, lies to him, and this creates discomfort at home.

If we were to ask the wife if she feels abandoned and isolated by her husband, she would probably answer "yes" to us. If we were to ask the husband if he feels there is a communication problem in his marriage, he would also probably say "yes" to us. What we have learned from their discussion is completely new information which allows us to re–cycle the "NO TRUST" issue into simple concepts of conflict differences. These concept differences are outlined below.

CONCEPTUAL DIFFERENCES	
Husband's Concept	Wife's Concept
Communication Problems	Abandonment & Isolation

The following diagram illustrates how we drill down for information and conceptualize that layer of information. This exploration is much like drilling for pockets of oil in various layers of the earth.

DRILLING FOR NEW MEANING

No Divorce Position

Lies to me
Home Life Uncomfortable
Argues with me

"No Trust" Issue

Divorce Position

Had an Affair
Stays at the Office
Doesn't Talk Anymore

Communication Problems ← Concept → Abandonment and Isolation

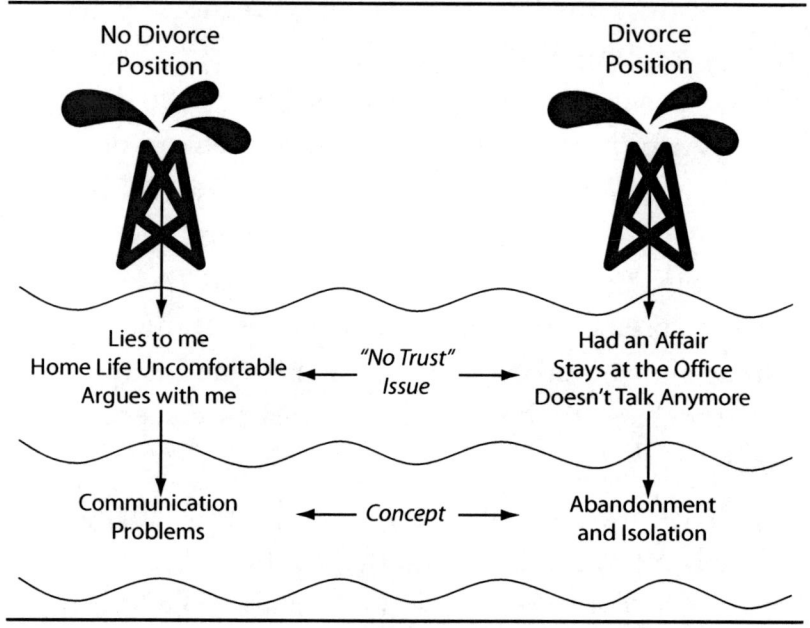

Diagram XVII – Drilling for New Meaning

Chapter Six

Lets go to the other issues and see what we can learn in discussion. The issue of "LOVE" for each other is set out below.

"Love" Issue

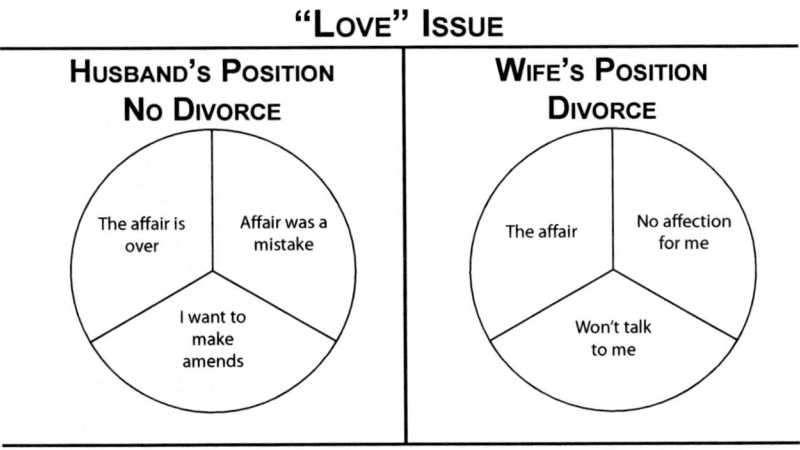

Husband's Position No Divorce	Wife's Position Divorce
The affair is over / Affair was a mistake / I want to make amends	The affair / No affection for me / Won't talk to me

Diagram XVIII – "Love" Issue

From the discussion of this issue we can presume that the husband feels blame and regret. The wife still feels abandoned and isolated.

We can re-frame or re-cycle this "LOVE" issue to look like these concepts.

CONCEPTUAL DIFFERENCES	
Husband's Concept	Wife's Concept
Blame and Regret	Abandonment & Isolation

The third issue of the husband's affair, and the wife's feelings as the result of this issue, has already been covered in the "LOVE" issue. Therefore, this hypothetical divorce boils down to the following new concepts.

Husband's Concepts	Wife's Concepts
1. Communications with wife	1. Abandonment by husband
2. Blame and regret for the affair	2. Isolation by husband

We now realize the real or perceived causes of the divorce from each spouses' perspective. By asking each party to disclose the parts and pieces of each issue and then adequately re-framing or conceptualizing them, we are able to simplify the conflict process. In truth, we re-cycle the issues to obtain additional new information and insights from the underlying reasons for the conflict. The issues are now transformed into new concepts which are true distinctions and differences.

In the Learn process we are constantly drilling down to get to the root of the problem. When we drill down and re-frame or re-cycle our conflict, the true differences between the parties are discovered. As seen in the last divorce illustration, some issues can be combined because they speak to the same root cause. The wife really wants the divorce solely because she feels isolated and abandoned by her husband. The husband on the other hand doesn't want the divorce; however, he must work out the issues of 1) communication with his wife and 2) the blame and regret of the affair. Both his communication style and blame appear to have caused the wife's feeling of abandonment. These differences will be addressed in the Understand block of the V.A.L.U.E. process. How to understand differences is fully explained in the next chapter.

Chapter Six

> **KEY POINT**
>
> **Reforming and Recycling**
>
> The goal of the Learn block is to discover the substantive meaning of each party's issues and recycle or transform that meaning into a new concept. This transformation is done by:
>
> 1. Asking each party to define in three parts what his issue means to him.
>
> (circle divided into three sections labeled "meaning", "meaning", "meaning")
>
> 2. If possible, combine meanings to determine one or more central themes and name that theme in no more than (7) seven words as a new concept.
> 3. Get each party's agreement of this new concept or phrase, and validate the concept.
> 4. Set up an agenda for discussion of these conceptual differences in the Understand block.

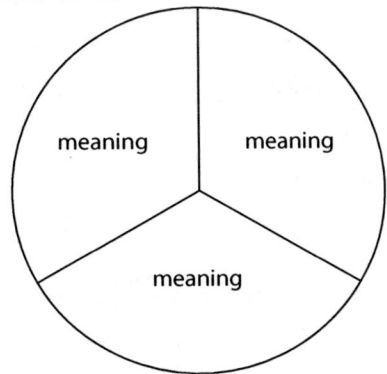

Let's look at another example of the Learn process, our husband and wife discussing the conflict over money

Seeing Through The Wall

spent on personal items. In Chapter V, both husband and wife outlined their positions and supporting beliefs or issues. We put it in outline form as below:

CONFLICT/DISCUSSION AGENDA	
Husband	Wife
<u>Position</u>: Too much money spent on personal items	<u>Position</u>: Money spent on personal items is necessary
<u>Beliefs or Issues</u>: 1. Too many shoes 2. Too many make-up items 3. Too many church dresses	<u>Beliefs or Issues</u>: 1. Need shoes for work 2. Stay in style 3. Need to look good socially

Following our process of Learn, both husband and wife would further define their reasons for their issues or beliefs. The husband's reasons would probably look like this for each of his issues:

HUSBAND

- Over our Budget
- Person is not judged by clothes
- You look great already

Diagram XIX – Husband's Reasons

Chapter Six

In analyzing these items we would get (1) the husband's value statement that people shouldn't be judged by what they wear, (2) a fact that the spending exceeds their budget, and (3) a perception that his wife looks great already.

Moving to the wife's issue of needing shoes for work, she reasons in the following manner:

WIFE

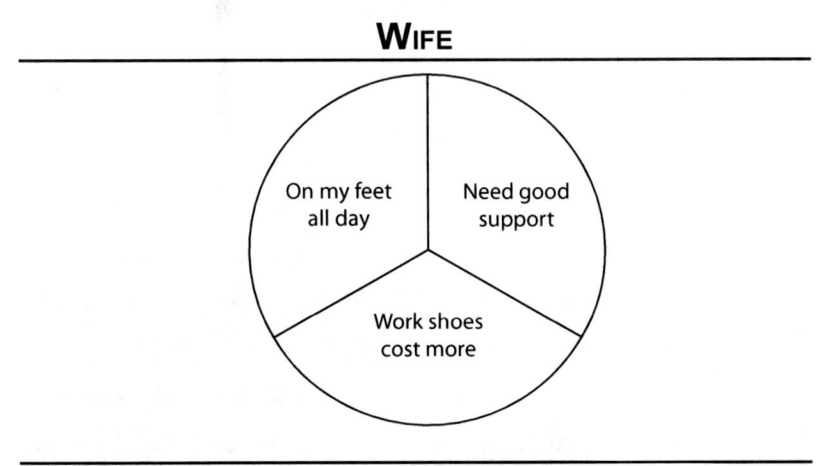

(Pie chart with three sections: "On my feet all day", "Need good support", "Work shoes cost more")

Diagram XX – Wife's Reasons

If we analyze these items we would get 1) a need for shoes with good support, 2) a fact or perception that good shoes cost more, and 3) a fact that she stands all day long. We can recycle this into a concept of a "health" issue. We can also combine the issues of staying in style and looking good since they are so similar.

WIFE

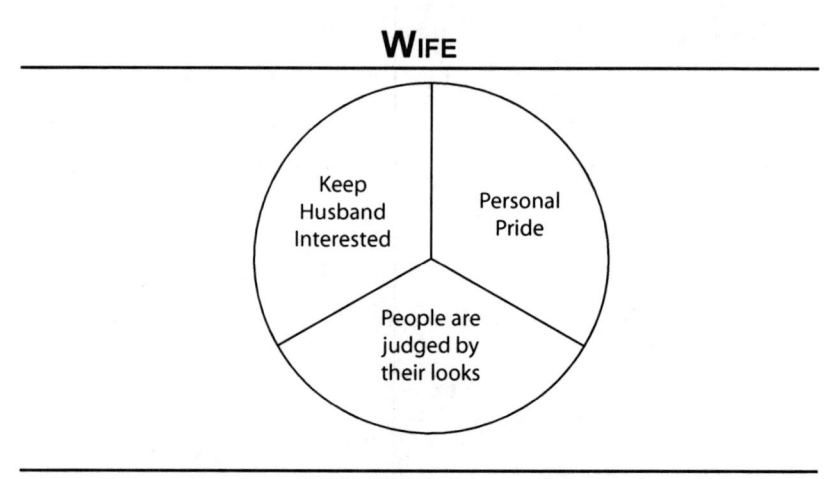

```
        Keep
        Husband        Personal
        Interested     Pride

            People are
            judged by
            their looks
```

Diagram XXI – Wife's Issues Recycled

From the above diagram, it appears there is (1) a need to be attractive both for personal and social reasons, and (2) a personal value to look good. The wife's reasons could be conceptualized as an "appearance" issue.

When we put these issues side by side we can determine the different concepts to be discussed in the Understand block of the system; however, for right now, the formation of the new and recycled issues is all we need. The comparison is shown next.

Chapter Six

TRANSFORMED ISSUES

HUSBAND

Budget Issue circle:
- Over our Budget
- Person is not judged by clothes
- You look great already

BUDGET ISSUE AND APPEARANCE ISSUE

WIFE

Health Issue circle:
- On my feet all day
- Need good support
- Work shoes cost more

"HEALTH" ISSUE

Appearance Issue circle:
- Keep Husband Interested
- Personal Pride
- People are judged by their looks

"APPEARANCE" ISSUE

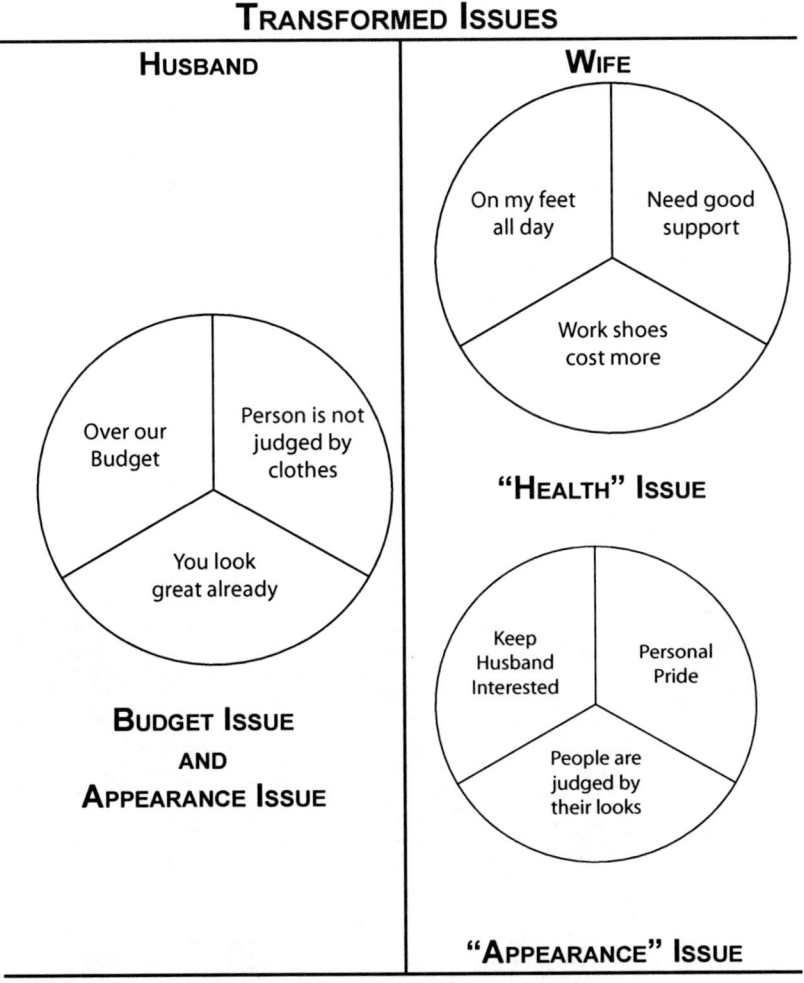

Diagram XXII – Transformed Issues

You probably noticed that when we looked at the reasons grouped above we attached a need, belief, value, perception, or fact to the meaning. If you can, it is helpful to "name" the meaning or reason. Naming helps you categorize each reason for the Understand block. As we discovered in Chapter IV, values are at the core of a person. Values are difficult to change. People really fight to maintain their personal values in conflict dialogue. On the other hand, a belief expressed as a perception or need can be altered or modified with dialogue. Try training yourself to recognize and name reasons. Simply ask yourself whether the conclusion of the statement sounds like a value, fact, perception, belief, or attitude This categorization is shown in the diagram below:

Chapter Six

CATEGORIZATION OF TRANSFORMED ISSUES

HUSBAND | **WIFE**

Husband circle (labeled *Fact or Belief*, *Value*, *Perception*):
- Over our Budget
- Person is not judged by clothes
- You look great already

Wife circle 1 (labeled *Fact*, *Need*, *Fact or Belief*):
- On my feet all day
- Need good support
- Work shoes cost more

Wife circle 2 (labeled *Need or Perception*, *Value*, *Value and Need*):
- Keep Husband Interested
- Personal Pride
- People are judged by their looks

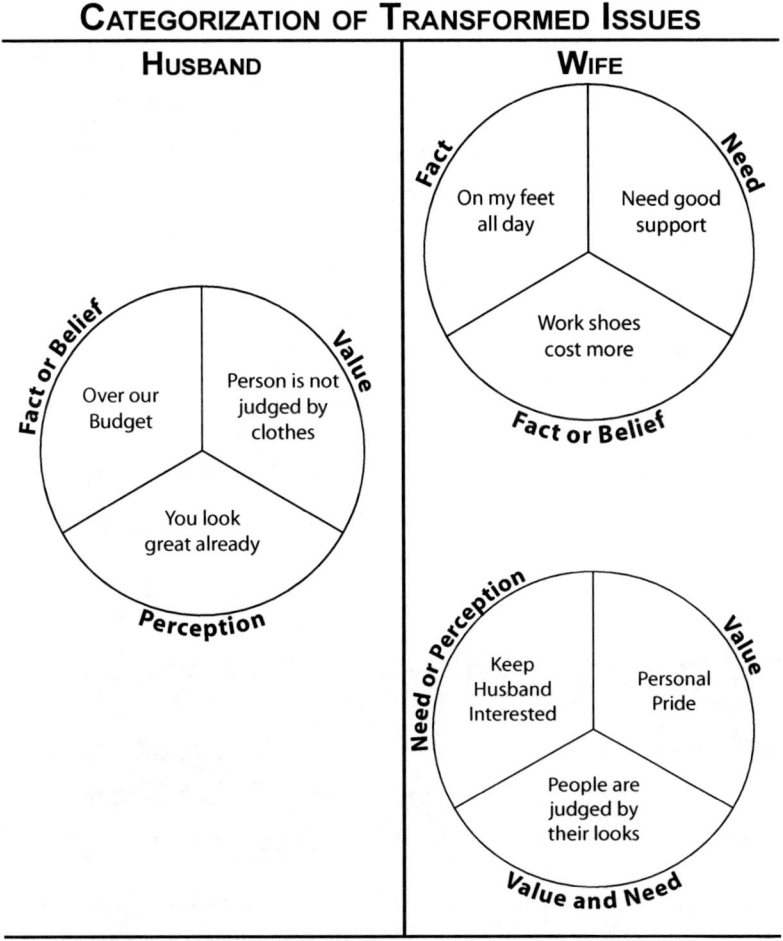

Diagram XXIII – Categorization of Transformed Issues

Because meanings represent values, beliefs, attitude, perception, needs, facts or other items, we need to recognize and learn how to utilize this concept of categorizing issues. For example, the "health" issue of the wife revolves around a health need and two facts or beliefs that demonstrate that need. Her "appearance" issue revolves around her value system and her perception or

125

need. On the husband's side we are dealing with mostly perceptions and beliefs and only one value statement. This delineation is important to know because we learn what motivates the meaning and get a glimpse of how to resolve the differences. If we look at what the meanings represent, we learn a new set of information (as outlined below) that may be contributing to the conflict.

Husband		Wife
Value: People are not judged by clothes	vs.	*Value:* People are judged by their looks *Value:* Personal pride
Perception: You look great already	vs.	*Perception or need:* Keep husband interested
Fact or Belief: Over our budget	vs.	*Fact:* On my feet all day *Fact:* Need good support *Fact or Belief:* Work shoes cost more

Looking at this conflict in another representation, we see the following pairing of values, beliefs, and attitudes.

Chapter Six

PARING OF VALUES, BELIEFS AND ATTITUDES

HUSBAND	WIFE
Perceptions or Attitudes: You look great already Beliefs or Facts: Over our budget VALUES: People not judged by clothes	Perceptions or Attitudes: Keep Husband Interested Beliefs or Facts: Work shoes cost more, On my feet all day, Need good support VALUES: People judged by looks, Personal pride

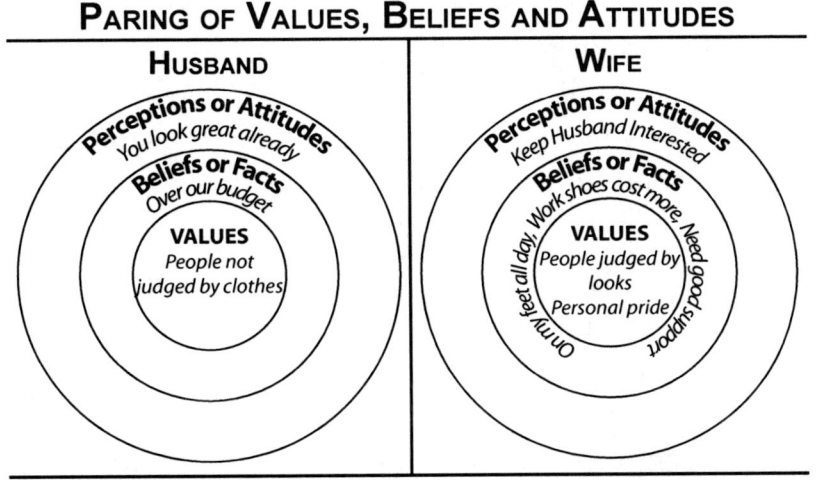

Diagram XXIV – Paring of Values, Beliefs and Attitudes

Basically in this family conflict we have a clash of values and facts (or beliefs). The perception concerning the husband's interest in the wife can be put aside because we learn the husband is interested in her and states so with his attitude of "You look great already." Therefore, the conflict centers around the differing values of the husband and wife. Because values are deeply ingrained via socialization, people find them difficult to change. If values are in conflict and cannot be changed, they must be strongly validated by each party. Strong validation (confirmation of values) will allow the parties to shift from a dialogue of values and concentrate on what can be discussed and negotiated ... the wife's health needs, and the family budget. These techniques will be more fully explored in the next chapter on Understanding.

Learning about the substantive issues is a process of drilling down, discovering meaning, conceptualizing issues, and naming the motivation. This is an educational process for both parties that enables them to see, hear, and feel the conflict in its full dimension. We learn when we ask, then think about and analyze the response. It helps learning to chart meanings out on paper or draw diagrams to aid visual recognition of the conflict.

Up to now we have only learned how the true conflict looks, sounds, and feels. The goal of our dialogue and discussions has been to discover the meaning of the issues, form concepts, (if possible) and determine the human motivation behind each issue's meaning. Hopefully we have gained insight into the true nature of the conflict or been able to combine or eliminate some issues in the process. However, if this last task did not happen that is all right. We still learned the meaning and the substance of the conflict to then Understand in the next block of the V.A.L.U.E. process.

Chapter Six

THE V.A.L.U.E. SYSTEM GUIDE

Concept	Definition	When to Use	Words to Use
LEARN	A four part process of re-defining the true multi-part substance of conflict issues. 1) Ask for the three main parts of each issue, and discuss these parts of each issue. 2) Next, find an equation or concepts that simplifies and matches the main thrust of the dialogue in 1) above. 3) Discover which statements are values, beliefs, needs, facts or perceptions for clarity and importance. 4) Discuss these ideas and concept to discover new information.	Use when it is necessary to learn the substance of another's position, issue, belief, value, or fact statement. Use the process in the Learn and Understand blocks of the V.A.L.U.E. system.	"I need to know more about your position or issue. Will you break it down into three simple parts for me?" – or – "I must have missed a part of your reasons for your position. What part or parts did I miss?" – or – "I sense there are other parts to your position. What part is missing that I would need to know?"

129

Chapter Seven

Any fool can know. The point is to understand.
Albert Einstein

V.A.L.U.E. BLOCK FOUR: HOW TO UNDERSTAND THE DIFFERENCES AND DISTINCTIONS

UNDERSTAND DISTINCTIONS AND DIFFERENCES

To Understand is the fourth block of the V.A.L.U.E. System. To understand means to logically discuss the distinctions and differences produced in the Learn block to obtain new information for resolution of the conflict. Specifically, the understand block: 1) explores the sub–parts of each new concept developed by each party, 2) combines sub–parts of particular issues which are similar, 3) looks for the similarities of each side's sub–parts for quick agreement, 4) compares and contrasts each side's sub–points, and 5) where the sub–parts differ asks what this difference means to each party as to the resolution of the conflict.

DISTINCTIONS AND DIFFERENCES

Most of us are taught to find what is similar in conflict and work on this common ground for resolution. This approach is not a bad philosophy; however, in today's world it does not always work because of our contemporary society. For example, differences exist, in attitudes, cultures, lifestyles, and gender. Increasingly there are fewer homogenous groups and more people with different value sets, attitudes, or beliefs. More often than not there are more differences than similarities in contemporary conflict.

KEY POINT

In the concept of the V.A.L.U.E. System, differences mean perceptions that are opposite. *Distinctions are different characteristics of the same concept ... the subparts.*

A major philosophy of this book is that resolution results through dialogue on the differences in concepts and distinctions in their subparts. In the context of the V.A.L.U.E. System, difference means not alike or opposite. For example, black and white, male or female, adult or child. On the other hand, distinctions are difference characteristics of the same concept. Distinctions define different characteristics of the same concepts, whereas differences seek to find opposite meanings to a concept. For example, the concept of love has many shades of meaning based upon an individual's perception. Distinctions and differences, properly discussed, allow a new understanding to emerge. Based upon this in–depth information individuals can say, "That's new information to me and something I did not know before we talked. Based upon this new information, I can resolve or settle this dispute right now." What is common ground will stay common ground for easy resolution; however, what is different must be fully explained to gain a new depth of understanding.

In the 21st century, working with conflict resolution means recognizing differences and having the skills to use them to attain resolution. For example, one couple I worked with had unique distinctions with no apparent logical reasoning on the issue of travel. The husband, Bill, traveled on business and thought nothing of leaving his wife Alice for days at a time. Although Bill hated to fly his job demanded it. Therefore he flew because he had to work. On the other hand when Alice wanted to fly to visit relatives Bill staunchly objected to her flying and leaving home for days. Of course Bill's position did not sound logical to Alice. However during the Understand block, Bill admitted he feared air crashes and also revealed he was left alone as a child by his parents for long periods of time. Once Alice understood these two pieces of new information she determined her husband had a deep seated fear of being abandoned by loved ones. Upon further discussion, it became apparent that Bill didn't object to his wife visiting relatives. He was fearful of Alice being killed in a plane crash and his being abandoned. Bill's fears were so strong that his position appeared stubborn and illogical. Validating the new information enabled the couple to resolve their conflict with greater clarity, and empowered Bill to seek professional help. Bill began to address his fear of abandonment with the help of a psychologist and his work/travel situation improved, and so did their marriage.

In another example, a divorcing couple could not decide how to divide their last asset, the dining room table and chairs. The couple explored all manner of options to no avail. I finally asked the wife, Laura, "What is the difference in this asset as opposed to the other assets?" Laura answered, "We bought this table and chairs together when we were first married. It was our first purchase together." Then I asked her, "What does this difference mean to you in this divorce?" Laura tearfully answered that this asset symbolized their marriage even thought it did not last. Hearing Laura's revelation the husband said, "She can have the table and chairs." Laura's statement empowered her husband enough to settle this matter, and the division of assets was over.

The goal of the Understand block is to obtain a new depth of information from the dialogue on differences. New information allows you to 1) fully understand the motivation of the other person, 2) gain background on the subject matter in controversy, 3) see any hidden perspectives, 4) allow a new position or thinking pattern to emerge, 5) use the information to "save face" in negotiating a resolution to a conflict, and most importantly 6) provide building blocks for the empowerment stage of the process.

Chapter Seven

At this point you may be thinking, "I understand what you are saying and it makes sense, but I am afraid to put such differences out in the open and talk about them. I may not be able to stay calm or the other person may get upset at me and shut the negotiation down." Remember the result of the validation at this juncture. All through this process validation of positions, issues, meanings, concepts, or other points has taken place. Also, parties have agreed to accept as accurate the validated points. Adequate validation will effectively eliminate defensive behavior because everyone's points have been acknowledged by others. No one person controls the process.

EXPLORING THE SUB–PARTS

When we explore the sub–parts of concepts formed in the Learn block, we enter a deeper level of meaning through dialogue. We are drilling deeper into these concepts to gain new, added meaning similar to our process in the Learn block. In our divorce example, the husband and wife need to dialogue on their concepts developed on in Chapter VI. The concepts are reproduced below.

Husband's Concepts	Wife's Concepts
1. Communications with wife	1. Abandonment by husband
2. Blame and Regret	2. Isolation by husband

The husband needs to outline for his wife the parts and pieces of their communication problem. He also needs to tell her the reason for blaming her, and acknowledge his

Seeing Through The Wall

regret over his affair. By the same process the wife needs to explain to her husband why she feels abandoned and isolated in their marriage. Their dialogue is diagrammed below.

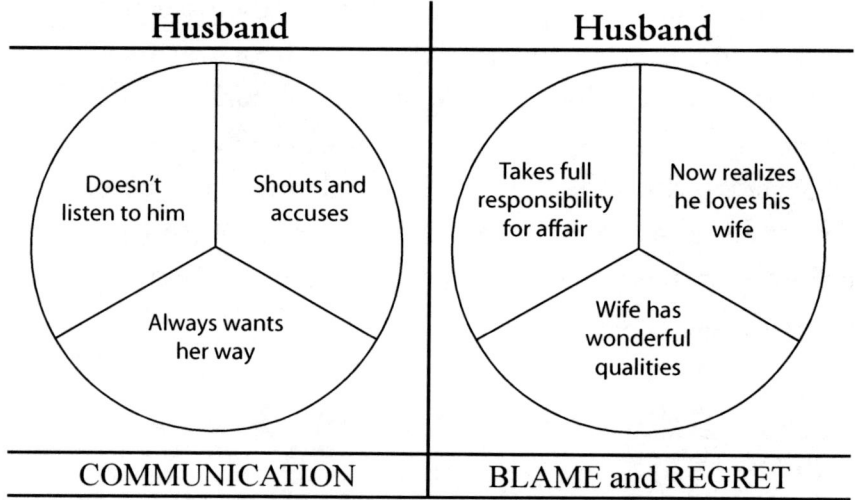

Husband | Husband

Husband (COMMUNICATION)	Husband (BLAME and REGRET)
Doesn't listen to him / Shouts and accuses / Always wants her way	Takes full responsibility for affair / Now realizes he loves his wife / Wife has wonderful qualities

Diagram XXV – Husband's Dialog

Wife | Wife

Wife (ISOLATION)	Wife (ABANDONMENT)
No calls from the office / No gifts or flowers / No quality communication	No showing of love / No family / No quality communication

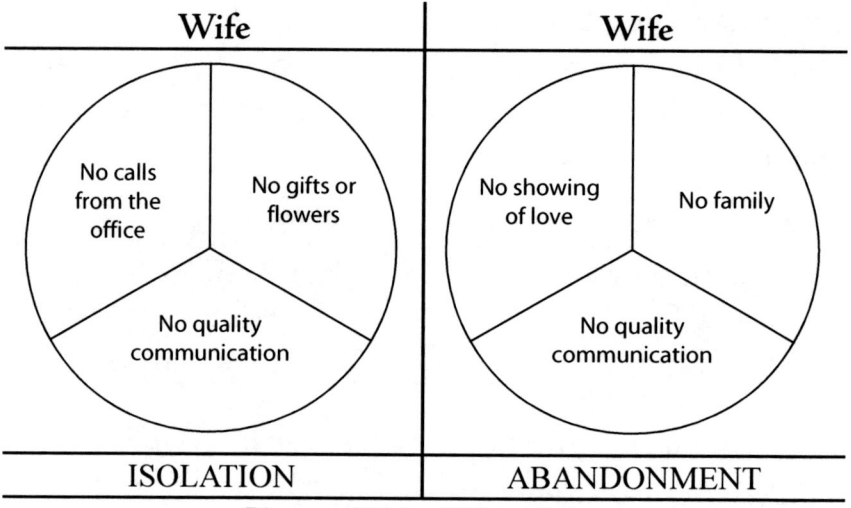

Diagram XXVI – Wife's Dialog

Chapter Seven

LOOK FOR THE SAME SUB-PARTS

In the divorce dialogue above, there are many sub-parts of the wife's concepts that sound alike and could be combined into concepts of isolation and abandonment. Now we can go deeper in meaning. All the sub-parts look like what the wife needs in her marriage. We can put the similar sub-parts together and re-name them as "Wife's Needs." Now we have what the wife needs in the marriage from her husband as follows.

Wife's Needs
1. Calls during the day
2. Gifts and flowers
3. A showing of love
4. Quality communication
5. A family

The husband also has a need for quality communication. If we were to name his need it appears to be "better behavior" on the part of the wife. Currently she behaves as though she doesn't listen, shouts, accuses, and demands her way.

CONTRAST THE SUB-PARTS

When we dialogue on the differences in the sub-parts of this divorce issue, we can represent it in the following manner.

Seeing Through The Wall

Contrasting Differences	
Husband	Wife
1. Wife needs to listen	1. Husband calls from office during the day
2. Wife needs to use a milder tone of voice	2. Husband shows love by: – Calls from office – Brings gifts & flowers – Wants to start a family
3. Wife wants her way	3. Family
4. Wife has wonderful qualities	4. ????????
5. Husband realizes he loves his wife	
6. Full responsibility for the affair	

Inquire About the Difference

From the listing of contrasting differences it appears only one difference is without some logical counterpoint. The husband states that he will take full responsibility for his affair, yet there is no direct counterpoint on the wife's side. This fact is a big difference and one that must be addressed. Addressing this issue is a critical point in this block of the process. Unless this difference is handled correctly and with the proper communication technique, the entire peaceful dialogue might explode into argument.

Chapter Seven

At this point in the dialogue we need only be concerned with what the husband's statement of full responsibility for the affair means to the wife. She is hearing his admission for the first time. It is new information. Asking "why" he takes full responsibility might plunge the dialogue backward into guilt and shame and put the husband on the defensive. To forward the dialogue at this point and advance the resolution, the husband needs to know whether this new revelation makes any difference to his wife. This difference would empower her to restore their marriage. The husband must say, "Wife, I take full responsibility for my affair. Knowing my acknowledgement, does it make any difference to you in this divorce proceeding? If so, please tell me."

The wife has two choices, "yes" or "no." If she says "yes" then she tells her husband why this new information makes a difference. If she says "no", it is a dead issue or moot point. Let's pretend the wife says "yes" and outlines her reasons below to be:

> 1. His admission of fault lets me know it wasn't my actions that drove him away
>   Also ...
> 2. He says I have wonderful qualities, and
> 3. The affair made him realize
>   he loves me after all

Asking what the difference MEANS to the other person requires a response that advances the dialogue with more, new information. What we learn is the wife felt the affair was due to her actions (or behavior), and that conclusion proved not to be true in this hypothetical case.

When we look at the other differences side by side, it appears the husband is also receiving new information concerning what his wife needs in their marriage. The wife needs to ask the same type of question to determine whether this new information will make any difference to her husband. The wife needs to say, "Husband, what I need to make our marriage work is attention from you. I would appreciate that in the form of flowers, gifts, calls during the day, and I would also like to start a family. Knowing this new information, does it make a difference to you in our divorce? If so, please tell me why." If the husband says "no" there will probably be a divorce; however, it will probably be more civil than before. More likely the husband will say "yes" and agree to meet his wife's expressed needs.

Still the issue of communication differences remains. Both husband and wife need to dialogue on the meaning of quality communication. However, with the isolation and abandonment issues partially resolved, the wife may agree to listen, keep a neutral tone of voice and not always have her way in discussions.

Chapter Seven

STRESS NEEDS, VALUES, BELIEFS AND PERCEPTIONS

When dialoguing on differences, it helps to stress the underlying motivation for the difference to the other person as you see it. The motivation could be a need, a want, a belief, a value, or a fact. Characterizing an issue as a belief, value, or fact acknowledges the manner in which you took the statement. Thus, the other party has the option of correcting the categorization which will further clarify the dialogue, especially a dialogue on differences. Let's assume the husband didn't see his wife's statements of no calls, gifts, flowers, or a family as needs but just wants. He might say, "I hear you want me to send you flowers and give you gifts." The wife then has an opportunity to clarify and say, "I don't just want them, I need them to show me your love, especially after your affair." Such clarity may truly be new information to the husband because he may not have realized the manner in which he needed to demonstrate his love for his wife and the depth of her need, considering his affair.

TRY TO MAKE AN EQUATION OF MEANING

During this Understand block, the more you can ascertain what a concept equals to a person the further you advance the dialogue. Remember in school math when we learned equations $x = y + 1$ or $5 + 3 = 8$. When we ask what this new information means to the other person we are asking for an equation of meaning. For example, in this divorce case "love" to the wife is shown in the following equation.

$$LOVE = CALLS + GIFTS + FLOWERS + FAMILY$$

To the husband, quality communication is shown in the following equation:

$$QUALITY\ COMMUNICATION = LISTENING + TONALITY + REASONABLENESS$$

Outlining and validating these equations is another way to express the differences in meaning. Such equations may make discussions easier for the parties to visualize differences. Achieving the equations is the process described in the Empowerment block of the V.A.L.U.E. System.

Let's take our other couple's conflict over spending on personal items, and apply the Understand process to their conflict. From the Learn block they have transformed their conflict into three major concepts of Budget, Health, and Appearance. The couple has also been able to name the values, facts, beliefs, perceptions, and attitudes of each sub–part in their conflict. These contrasting sub–parts are set out below like they were presented in Chapter VI.

Chapter Seven

Husband		Wife
Value: People are not judged by clothes	vs.	**Value:** People are judged by their looks **Value:** Personal pride
Perception: You look great already	vs.	**Perception or need:** Keep husband interested
Fact or Belief: Over our budget	vs.	**Fact:** On my feet all day **Fact:** Need good support **Fact or Belief:** Work shoes cost more

We can now put these sub-parts from the perspective of human values, beliefs, and perceptions under their proper concepts of Budget, Health, and Appearance. . If we look at the conflict in this manner we can contrast the full difference as follows:

Husband		Wife
Budget	vs.	Health
Fact or Belief: Over our budget	vs.	**Fact:** On my feet all day **Fact:** Need good support **Fact or Belief:** Work shoes cost more

Husband		Wife
Appearance	vs.	Appearance
Value: People are not judged by clothes	vs.	**Value:** People are judged by their looks **Value:** Personal pride
Perception: You look great already	vs.	**Perception or need:** Keep husband interested

Although the husband and wife may choose to discuss budget, health, or appearance, the "appearance" issue is common to both; therefore, easier to discuss first. Note the underlying motivations for this issue ... values and perceptions (or needs). As mentioned previously in

Chapter Seven

Chapter VI, values are deeply ingrained and socialized. It is as though values are hard-wired into our brains as we grow into adulthood. Values are difficult to negotiate because people perceive they will have to surrender their values within the negotiation. To overcome this resistance, values must be recognized and validated. The husband needs to say, "I hear you expressing a value of personal pride in looking good because you feel people are judged by their looks. Is that right?" Of course, the wife will answer "yes" to this proper validation. The husband can then say, "I would like to add to this discussion my value. I feel people are not judged by their clothes. Can we discuss this?"

Within this discussion more new information is exposed. The wife explains to her husband her theory of sales to medical professionals. In her business she perceives the following equation matters.

$$\text{Good appearance for successful selling} = \text{Professional looking business clothes} + \text{shoes} + \text{make-up}$$

She stresses to her husband how first appearances make a difference in her line of medical sales. She needs to make a visual impression on the doctors who have little time to meet with medical sales representatives.

The wife is giving her husband a distinction based upon her work, not on her personal whims. The husband can "save face" and say, "I never thought of your appearance in that way. You always look good to me."

The wife can then validate her husband's response and affirm she perceives a need to look good to keep her husband interested in her. If the husband is smart he will perceive her validation as a need for re-assurance and then re-assure her she always looks great to him whatever she is wearing.

Now, the conflict boils down to the Budget vs. Health issues. However, the husband received new information from the last discussion on the appearance issue. His wife needs a great appearance in her medical sales position. Based upon the new insight, the wife can say, "Husband, knowing my needs in sales presentations, does this make a difference with our budget discussion?" Logically, the husband would say "yes" and the wife then says "OK, let's talk about the budget."

Within this next discussion there is no need to talk about facts or beliefs as the wife's business needs have already been established and validated. How to budget for a good, professional appearance is the only issue. Upon drilling deeper into this issue the following sub-points may come out on each side as graphed below.

Chapter Seven

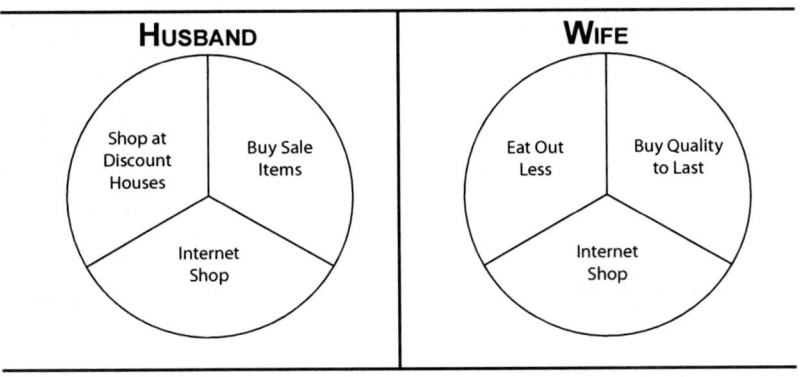

HUSBAND	WIFE
Shop at Discount Houses / Buy Sale Items / Internet Shop	Eat Out Less / Buy Quality to Last / Internet Shop

Diagram XXVII – Budget Sub Points

Notice the sub–points have the commonality of ways to save money when shopping for the wife's professional needs. We could actually change the "vs." to "and" which would give us a list of ways to stay within their budget. This list is set out below.

> **Ways to Stay Within Our Budget**
> 1. Shop the Internet
> 2. Shop at discount houses
> 3. Buy:
>   – sales items
>   – quality items that last
> 4. Eat out less

At this point, the husband and wife have successfully navigated through the Understand block. They have developed the necessary new information to use in the next block of Empower.

As demonstrated with two illustrations, the Understand block is designed to allow the parties to alter their previous thinking by consciously analyzing new information and "saving face." As illustrated, new information allows parties to 1) see new options to get their interest satisfied, 2) see new ways to let the other party win on an issue that was not so important to them in order to get a win or an issue that is vital to their interest, 3) claim a face–saving technique of saying, "Knowing the new information that you just disclosed, I can resolve this matter."

Dealing with Hidden Agendas or Resistance

If at this phase no options come forth for resolution or a party appears to resist dialogue, then probably a hidden issue or agenda is operating. In addition, the parties may have neglected or not validated an issue or sub–point. One party must ask the other, "What have I missed?" Upon disclosure and validation of the missing issue or sub–point, the parties can back up and recycle that issue through the Understand block then move forward to Empowerment.

If there is still conflict on an issue or issues then one party needs to ask, "What would you like to do now?" Keep quiet and let the other party think about the question and answer the question. Do not talk! Put the pressure on the other party to decide and answer. Most often, the answer will be an idea to resolve the issue or the need to discuss or bring up a new issue to be recycled as mentioned before. It is only after all issues and their sub–parts have been placed on the table for discussion, that all of the final options for resolution appear.

If resistance to dialogue appears, the following are some key questions to ask yourself or the other person.

1. Have I properly validated everything? If not, what do I need to validate?
2. What have I missed? – A hidden agenda or issue? If so, have I asked for it to be stated by asking, "What have I missed?"
3. Have I asked, "What would you like to do now … knowing all the information we have discussed?"

A majority of the time the answers to these key questions will jump start the dialogue, and put the process back on track.

Discovering the true meaning of difference is the real key to conflict resolution. The meaning of differences is critical to the other person. Only through discovery of new meaning can there be truthful dialogue that results in new knowledge for resolution of conflict.

An Observation on the Process

By now you have noticed that we use a similar process to drill down for more detailed information and advance the process. We treat positions, issues, and concepts like small boxes of Valentine candy. We open each box to see what's inside and then we dialogue to form a new concept or set up a new agenda for discussion.

Seeing Through The Wall

When my wife and I were in Russia, we were fascinated with the beautifully painted nesting dolls. Upon opening the top part of the wooden doll, a smaller wooden doll appears. Repeating this process, one finally gets to the last doll, a very small and beautifully decorated figure of a tiny girl. The Learn and Understand blocks are like opening Russian nesting dolls. Repeatedly opening information until there is no new information left to discuss, we then dialogue about what is inside to form a new concept or set up a new agenda for discussion. At the end of this, we reach the point of discussion of options for resolution.

Chapter Seven

THE V.A.L.U.E. SYSTEM GUIDE

Concept	Definition	When to Use	Words to Use
UNDERSTAND	A three part process of: 1) A comparison of the distinctions and differences between two conflicting concepts or issues. 2) Also, a further LEARN process to drill down and more fully explore the substance of the differences to bring out more new information for resolution options. 3) Asking if the distinctions and differences (in the form of new information) are enough for the other person to resolve the conflict.	Where within a dialogue differences and distinction are evident and apparent as new or different information that was not there before. Also use when new or different information would allow the other party to resolve the conflict because he or she has discovered new information that allows "face–saving" on his part or new options for resolution.	1. "I see that there are differences in the following issues. Can we discuss these differences?" 2. Use the Learn block as a guide to discussing and obtaining more new information. 3. "Knowing this new information about our issues, does this new information allow you to resolve our conflict?" Then, recycle the Understand block. 4. "Can we discuss why this new information doesn't make a difference in resolving this conflict?"

Chapter Eight

What may appear as the truth to one person will often appear as untruth to another person. But that need not worry the seeker. Where there is honest effort, it will be realized that what appeared to be different truths are like the countless and apparently different leaves of the same tree

Gandhi

V.A.L.U.E. BLOCK FIVE: HOW TO EMPOWER

Empower Resolution

Empower means to use the information gained in the Understand block to effectuate a resolution of the conflict including deciding on the steps necessary to activate a resolution plan for the future. During this block the options achieved in the Understand block are actualized. Many times an empowerment plan is written to formalize the resolution or aid parties to remember the timing of specific future plans. The empowerment plan can be very simple or as detailed as a policy, business agreement, or parenting plan in a divorce situation.

Resolution demands no written plan, however, writing out a plan helps crystallize the thinking of both parties and prevent "buyers remorse" after the discussions are completed.

How to Empower Resolution

A solution and a resolution differ within the context of the V.A.L.U.E. System – a solution is the answer or final disposition of a problem. Many times, only looking for a final disposition implies a negotiation tug–of–war where each side pulls as hard as she can to get what she needs based upon her original position. Normally the party with the most power wins because the negotiation tug–of–war is played on a continuum of 0% to 100% on each side. Joint problem solving or any information exchange is very limited. There is little or no V.A.L.U.E. in this negotiation process. On the other hand, where the emphasis is upon the issues, and not the positions of the parties, resolution of these underlying issue can take place … as in the V.A.L.U.E. System. A resolution looks at the underlying explanation for the problem and works with the substantive issues that form the conflict. The focus of the resolution is on joint discussion and problem solving, not on getting a final disposition. In the following diagram we see that both Party A and Party B are pulling against each other in a negotiation tug–of–war. Each is pulling toward their side to accomplish as much as possible in the negotiation. As depicted, Party A received 70% of his desired needs while Party B only received 30% of his needs. By inference, Party B will leave the negotiation

Chapter Eight

unhappy with only 30% of his needs met in the transaction. Later he might have some remorse or guilt because of the manner in which he negotiated the result. In a worst case scenario, Party B would back out of the deal.

A TYPICAL NEGOTIATION
(A NEGOTIATION TUG OF WAR)

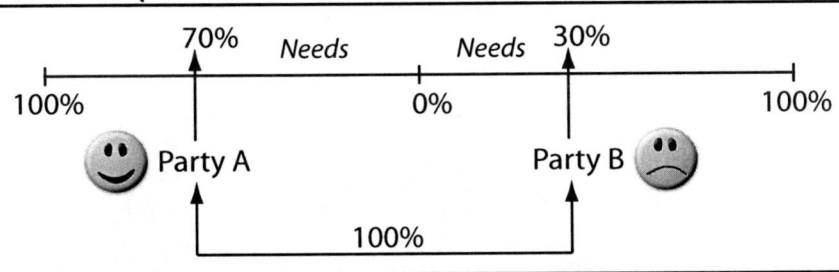

Diagram XXVIII – A Typical Negotiation "Tug of War"

To resolve a conflict it is best to change the dynamics of the negotiation game. Through the V.A.L.U.E. System, we change the dynamics of the discussions. We attempt to drill down and both Learn and Understand as much as possible about the other party's needs. Only then can we dialogue our differences to come up with face–saving options or options born out of new information from each party. The diagram below shows a new dynamic of working in a new manner to satisfy the true needs of each party. Instead of pulling against each other, both parties head in an new direction. Both parties dialogue about their needs, learn, and understand the differences. They both pull in the same direction which leads to more options that achieve most of what they desire.

A NEW RESOLUTION DYNAMIC

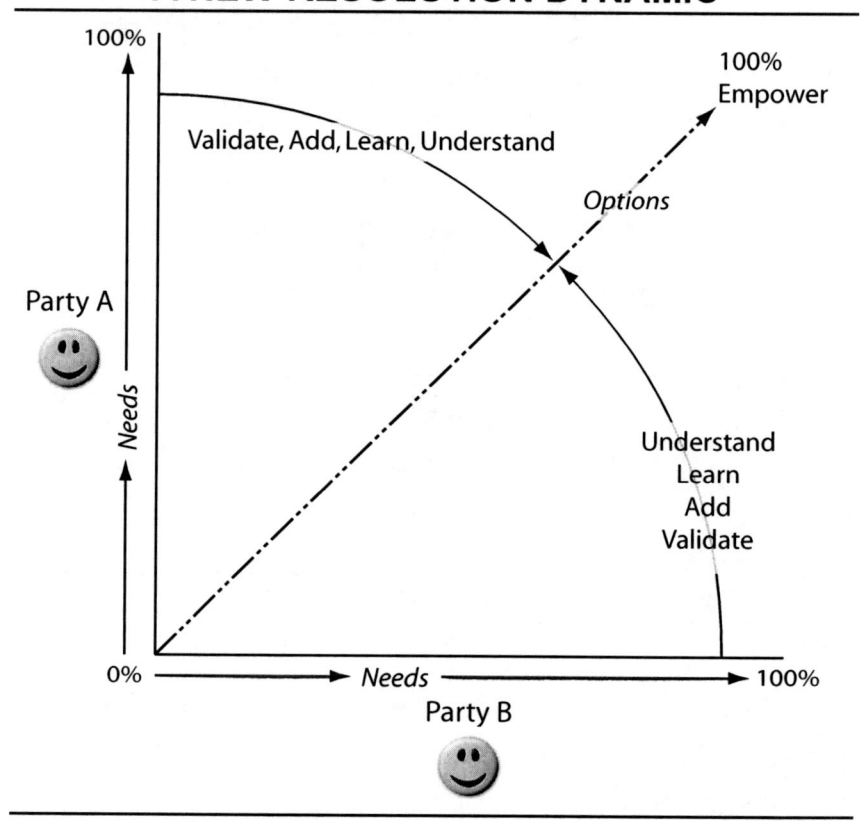

Diagram XXIX– Empowered Resolution

In the Understand block, we were able to reconcile difference between parties with more new information. Such information made enough difference to allow the parties options for resolution. For example, our husband and wife reconciled their spending based upon the wife's job needs. Then they focused upon ways to save money as options for complete resolution of their monetary budget conflict.

Our reconciled divorcing couple discussed their differences logically and discovered the true needs each person had in their current marital situation. These needs become options for resolution. In both cases, each party did not necessarily get what he wanted, but what he needed to resolve the matter. Empowerment is achieved when both parties are satisfied that their issues are addressed, and they get what they need to resolve the conflict at this time. If we look at the following diagram, we see that each party has achieves his desired goal in this resolution. Each has climbed up the blocks to where both are in the range of 80% to 100% satisfaction with their resolution.

A NEW WAY TO ACHIEVE 100%

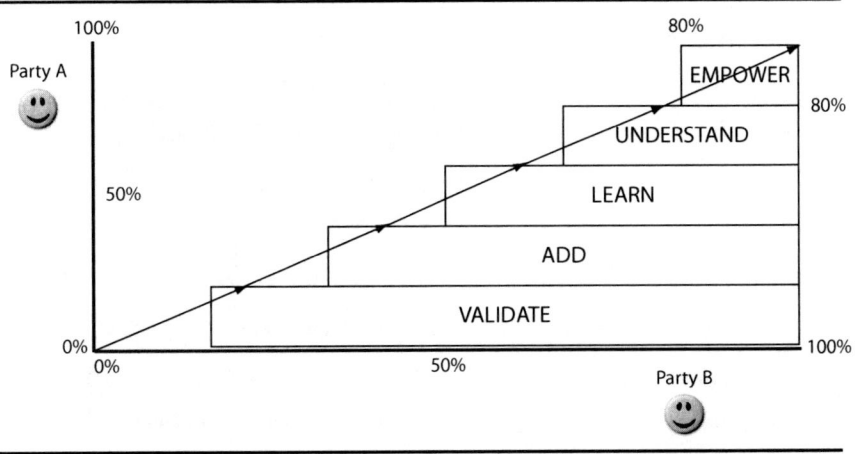

Party A — 100%, 50%, 0%
Party B — 0%, 50%, 100%

Steps: VALIDATE, ADD, LEARN, UNDERSTAND, EMPOWER (80%)

Diagram XXX – A New Way to Achieve 100%

With the V.A.L.U.E. System both parties move together in a new direction towards their goals. The result of this new direction allows both to achieve more of what they need. As they move up the building blocks, each step puts them closer to a resolution. Each party is validating, listening, discussing, dialoguing, and drilling for new information that will make a difference in resolution of this conflict. Such differences birth new options for resolution. Both parties climb in a new direction together, instead of pulling toward their individual 100% goals. Each party ends up in a new place where each receives from 80% to 100% of what he needs to resolve his conflict.

KEY POINT

A solution and a resolution differ within the context of the V.A.L.U.E. System. A solution is the answer or final disposition of a problem. Many times, only looking for a final disposition, implies a negotiation tug-of-war where each side pulls as hard as she can to get what she needs based upon her original position. A resolution looks at the underlying explanation for the problem and works with the substantive issues that form the conflict. The focus of the resolution deals with joint discussion and problem solving, not on negotiation techniques to achieve a final disposition or solution. Solution implies negotiation, and resolution implies joint in depth problem solving.

The Empowerment Plan

Once both parties reach the Empower block, they will activate the options achieved from the Understand

Chapter Eight

block within an Empowerment Plan. A general plan is outlined below. The parties can fill in the details from their Understand discussions. Such a plan covers all the bases and provides a working framework of actions to follow after the resolution of the conflict.

AN EMPOWERMENT PLAN OUTLINE

Either party can take the initiative to engage the other person in completing the action plan outlined below. It is as simple as saying, "Now that we have our new options, let's see how they play out in real life. Let's be specific and fill out the empowerment plan below."

> 1. Who will participate
> 2. What will be done by each participant
> 3. When will the actions take place
> 4. Where will the actions take place
> 5. How will the action be executed

In the case of our divorcing couple who are now reconciled, a simple empowerment plan might look like the following:

Seeing Through The Wall

AN EMPOWERMENT PLAN FOR THE RECONCILED COUPLE	
Who: Husband	**Who:** Wife
What: 1. Call wife from the office 2. Bring gifts and flowers home 3. Start a family	**What:** 1. Listen without interruption to my husband 2. Use a friendly tone of voice 3. Be practical about what I want 4. Start a family
When: 1. Calls during each business day 2. Flowers and gifts at last two times a month 3. Start a family or start adoption proceedings by year end	**When:** 1. In communication with my husband 2. When I am frustrated 3. When our budget demands attention 4. Start adoption procedure by year end if not pregnant by then
Where: At home and office	**Where:** At home and socially
How: Make notes in my appointment book and leave the office earlier to come home	**How:** Be aware of how I sound to others and exercise more to control my weight and frustrations

Chapter Eight

The empowerment plan for our couple to stay within a budget could be like the one outlined below.

BUDGET EMPOWERMENT PLAN
Who: Husband and Wife
What: Stay within our monthly budget
When: Every month except December
Where: At home with monthly accounting of our bank account balance
How: 1. Shop on the Internet for lower cost on quality goods   2. Shop at discount houses for overstocked items   3. Buy only sale items   4. Buy quality clothes and footwear that is professional looking   5. Eat out only once per week to save $250.00 per month for personal items

Simply having a written plan is empowering in and of itself. The plan actualizes the resolution while making both parties think in some detail about how they are going to accomplish the resolution. During the writing of the empowerment plan issues may come up that were not discussed before. Simply follow the V.A.L.U.E. system as outlined to discuss these issues, and add the new resolution to the existing empowerment plan.

Non-Resolution

If both parties climb up to the Understand block and cannot find enough new information for options for total resolution there may be a non-resolution. Many a non-resolution is caused by a "hidden agenda" of one party that was never disclosed and discussed within the process. One party is hiding a key piece of information that makes a difference in settlement to that party. Looking back, even asking the key question, "What have I missed?" didn't pull the hidden agenda out. At this point, one could ask, "Is there anything else we need to discuss?" This question might pull the "hidden agenda" out into the open. If so, work the "hidden agenda" through the V.A.L.U.E. System and hopefully there will be options for a good resolution. If not, then ask, "What would you like to do now?" and dialogue on the answer. One answer could be a "truce" with a revisit at a later time.

Re-Visiting the Conflict at a Later Time – "Truce"

One party may not be ready to resolve the conflict at this particular time. He may need more time to think and analyze the options. Also, he may need to consult with professional third parties. He also could feel a need to consult with family or trusted friends for re-assurance. The reasons are as varied as the personal situation.

It is unwise to press for a decision, as that would only make the other party defensive. Validate the need for more time, and discuss the terms of a "truce". Plan a time to re-visit the conflict and dialogue on options.

Within the "truce" plan, agree to use the V.A.L.U.E. process again, if needed. Otherwise the other party may simply need time to think, analyze, and dialogue with trusted advisors.

Walking Away with Dignity and Self-Worth

Regardless if there was a resolution, no resolution or a "truce", both parties will walk away from the conflict with dignity and self-worth. Throughout the V.A.L.U.E. System each party has been Validated as well as his values, beliefs, attitudes, needs, and perceptions. Neither party has been depreciated in the process of negotiation.

Each party has Learned and Understood the other party in a new and different way through working the V.A.L.U.E. process. Such a process fosters more peaceful relationships between these individuals in the future. Each party has learned a peaceful process for conflict resolution. Also, each person now has learned a new process for conflict resolution with others. Soon each person down the chain will be utilizing a conflict resolution process that allows individuals to engage and manage conflict properly in their everyday lives.

THE V.A.L.U.E. SYSTEM GUIDE

Concept	Definition	When to Use	Words to Use
EMPOWER	A process of putting together options from the Understand block and working–up an Empowerment Plan	Use the options produced from the discussion of distinctions and differences. Use these options to write an empowerment plan. Warning: Do not enter this Block until all issues have been discussed in the other Blocks, or Empowerment will be premature since some issues will most likely be left out.	"Considering this new information, I can settle the conflict by (state your options based upon the new information)." – or – "Knowing this new information, can we settle this dispute with [state your options based upon the new information]". – or – "Knowing this new information, I can settle based upon this information. Is that agreeable with you?"

Chapter Nine

*I do not want the peace that passeth understanding.
I want the understanding which bringeth peace*
Helen Keller

THE V.A.L.U.E. GUIDE

The following diagram is an overview of the major components of the V.A.L.U.E. System. It outlines the major steps necessary to climb the block to resolution of your conflict.

Following the diagram is a written guide to the V.A.L.U.E. System broken down into its component parts. The Guide outlines the definition of each block, when to use that particular block, and more importantly the exact words to use. Of course these words can be adapted to your particular speech style as you see fit. Just be sure you get to the meat or heart of each expression.

Seeing Through The Wall

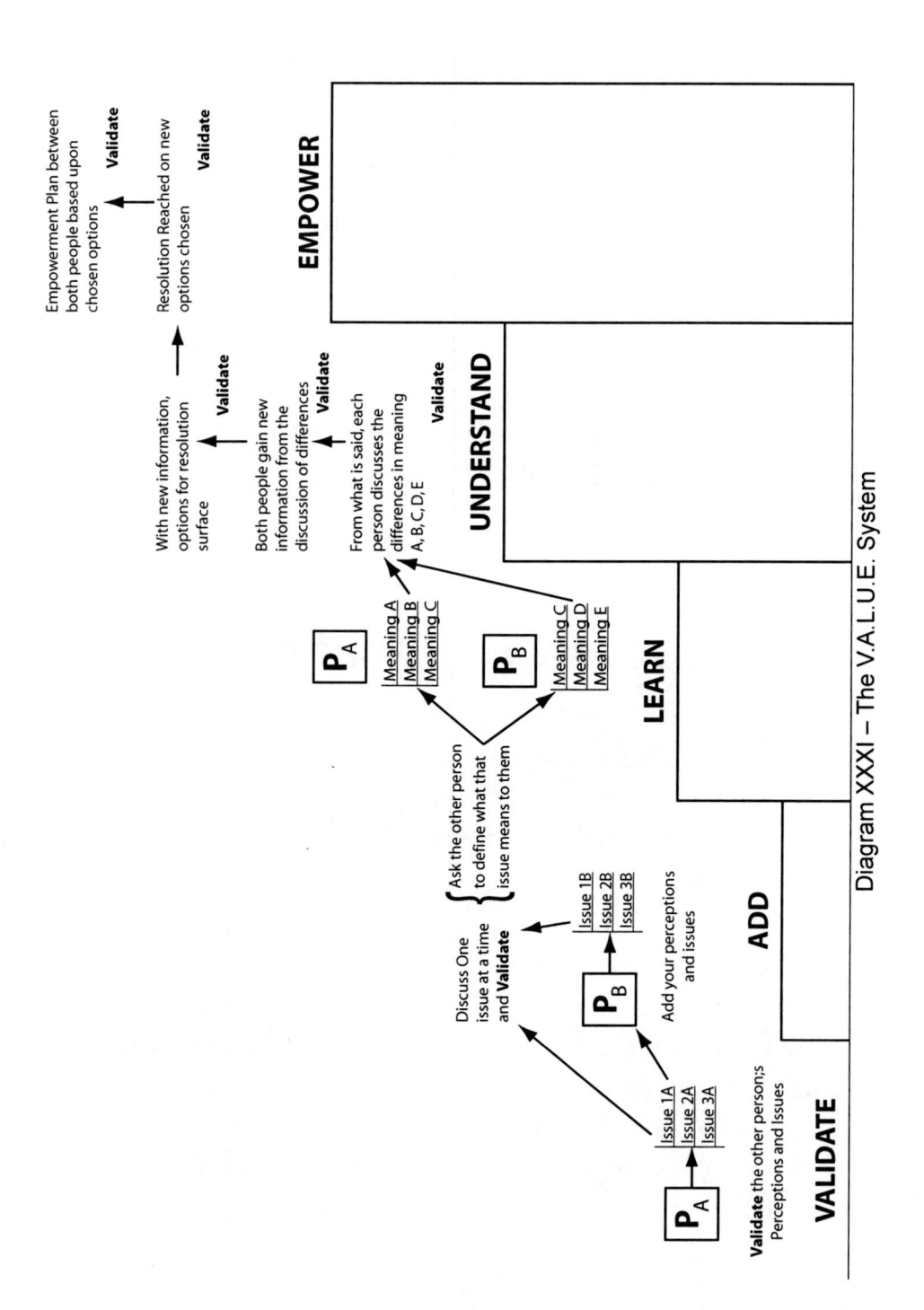

Diagram XXXI – The V.A.L.U.E. System

166

Chapter Nine

THE V.A.L.U.E. SYSTEM GUIDE

Concept	Definition	When to Use	Words to Use
VALIDATE	A communication technique which assures another person they have been fully heard, and acknowledged. The communication acknowledges them as a person, and also their ideas. Validation does not equal agreement with the other person or his ideas. Validation acknowledges a *right* to be a unique person and express your own ideas.	At every opportunity to confirm and acknowledge the other person or his perspective. Validation is used throughout every block of the system.	"I hear you say (then repeat what they said as closely to their exact words as possible). Then ask, "Is that correct?", or "Did I get that right?" If I didn't get it right, I ask, "What is right?" When they respond, repeat what they said and affirm your restatement as correct.

Seeing Through The Wall

THE V.A.L.U.E. SYSTEM GUIDE

Concept	Definition	When to Use	Words to Use
ADD	A communication strategy to validate the other person's perspectives or belief's, then to ADD your own perceptions, values, beliefs, attitudes or ideas.	Every time you need to ADD your perspective to any discussion or dialogue.	"I hear you are saying (Repeat the perspective), and I would like to ADD my perspective. My perspective is [then state your perspective]. CAVEAT: Never use the "yes, but" expression as the language discounts what the other person presented. The expression implies "yes, but my ideas are better."

Chapter Nine

THE V.A.L.U.E. SYSTEM GUIDE

Concept	Definition	When to Use	Words to Use
LEARN	A four part process of re-defining the true multi-part substance of conflict issues. 1) Ask for the three main parts of each issue, and discuss these parts of each issue. 2) Next, find an equation or concepts that simplifies and matches the main thrust of the dialogue in 1) above. 3) Discover which statements are values, beliefs, needs, facts or perceptions for clarity and importance. 4) Discuss these ideas and concept to discover new information.	Use when it is necessary to learn the substance of another's position, issue, belief, value, or fact statement. Use the process in the Learn and Understand blocks of the V.A.L.U.E. system.	"I need to know more about your position or issue." Will you break it down into three simple parts for me? – or – "I must have missed a part of your position. What part or parts did I miss? – or – "I sense there are other parts to your position. What part is missing that I would need to know?"

Seeing Through The Wall

THE V.A.L.U.E. SYSTEM GUIDE

Concept	Definition	When to Use	Words to Use
UNDERSTAND	A three part process of: 1) A comparison of the distinctions and differences between two conflicting concepts or issues. 2) Also, a further LEARN process to drill down and more fully explore the substance of the differences to bring out more new information for resolution options. 3) Asking if the distinctions and differences (in the form of new information) are enough for the other person to resolve the conflict.	Where within a dialogue differences and distinction are evident and apparent as new or different information that was not there before. Also use when new or different information would allow the other party to resolve the conflict because he or she has discovered new information that allows "face–saving" on his part or new options for resolution.	1. "I see that there are differences in the following issues. Can we discuss these differences?" 2. Use the Learn block as a guide to discussing and obtaining more new information. 3. "Knowing this new information about our issues, does this new information allow you to resolve our conflict?" Then, recycle the Understand block. 4. "Can we discuss why this new information doesn't make a difference in resolving this conflict?"

Chapter Nine

THE V.A.L.U.E. SYSTEM GUIDE

Concept	Definition	When to Use	Words to Use
EMPOWER	A process of putting together options from the Understand block and working–up an Empowerment Plan	Use the options produced from the discussion of distinctions and differences. Use these options to write an empowerment plan. Warning: Do not enter this Block until all issues have been discussed in the other Blocks, or Empowerment will be premature since some issues will most likely be left out.	"Considering this new information, I can settle the conflict by (state your options based upon the new information)". – or – "Knowing this new information, can we settle this dispute with [state your options based upon the new information]". – or – "Knowing this new information, I can settle based upon this information. Is that agreeable with you?"

Chapter Ten

*It is better to know some of the
questions than all the answers*
James Thurber

ILLUSTRATIONS OF THE V.A.L.U.E. SYSTEM

The V.A.L.U.E. System in Personal Interactions

After a wonderful birthday dinner for my wife, our hostess Betty, asked a senior pilot friend, "Why does your airline give estimated flying times that are always 30 minutes off schedule. You know how much I fly, and I always have to add 30 minutes to the flying time ... it never fails." Rich, the senior pilot, automatically became defensive because of Betty's verbal tone of blaming Rich for flight delays. He answered, "I don't know." This answer made Betty press harder in response and say, "Really, Rich, why do they do that!" Pressed again, Rich said, "The times are only estimates." To this comment Betty replied, "Then why don't they increase their estimates by 30 minutes?" Defensive again, Rich replied, "I don't know!"

At this point I stepped in with the V.A.L.U.E. System and began climbing up the building blocks.

Validate

I said, "Betty I need to validate your perception that the airline gives estimated flying times that are 30 minutes too short. Is that right?" To this Betty said, "Thank you!" I said, "Also that fact irritates you as a frequent flyer."

Betty replied, "Yes, it really does. I think they should be more accurate."

Add

I said to Rich, "Rich you would like to add to this discussion that the flying times are only estimates. Is that right?"

Rich answered, "Of course, that's why they are called 'estimated.' There are many variables in flying."

Learn

I said to Betty, "Betty, please tell me three reasons this airline procedure irritates you.

Betty replied:
1. I change planes a lot

2. I am on a tight schedule
3. Airlines should be more honest with passengers

I said to Rich, "Rich, I am sure there are more than three variables to flying time. Could you tell me the three most important."

Rich said:

1. Weather changes
2. Air speed and traffic
3. Forced delays

Understand

I said, "It sounds like Betty has business reasons for wanting airline honesty."

I also said, "It appears that Rich is saying there are variables in flight a pilot can't anticipate or control all the time."

Having been validated, Rich added, "The onboard system gives us the flying time. The computer can't predict the variables which could occur at the beginning or during the flight."

To this Betty said, "Oh, I didn't know you got the flying time that way. Just accurate at the start."

Rich then said, "Yes."

Empower

Betty then replied, "Oh well, I suppose the pilots are honest at the start of the flight, and I can't complain about that."

Rich answered with, "Thanks for saying your friend is honest. Just keep your 30 minutes as a safety margin for the variables."

Chapter Ten

The V.A.L.U.E. System in Consumer Affairs

Often consumers are not satisfied with the service they receive from providers. Disputes arise over charges, quality of services rendered, or misunderstandings of what needs to be repaired or replaced. In the following example, a car owner took his car in for a "trip–check" as the family was going on a road trip. The owner asked for the "trip–check" which included a diagnostic and physical check of the car's safety and operational capacity. He signed the authorization form and asked to be called before any major repairs were performed. When he picked up his car the bill was over $500.00. The dealership had charged him not only for the "trip–check" and minor costs of labor and parts, but also for a new break job. He received no call before the break repair and was very upset about the final cost. Using the V.A.L.U.E. System, the dialogue would progress as follows.

Dealership Manager, "Mr. Brown, you signed the authorization form for all repairs on your car that were shown to be needed by the 'trip–check.' We did the needed repairs for you and the cost is accurate."

Validate

Mr. Brown, Consumer, "I hear you say that I signed the authorization form and the repair cost is accurate. Is that correct?"

Manager, "Yes, you heard me correctly."

Add

Mr. Brown, "I need to add to what you said that I requested a call if there were to be any major repairs. I consider a break job a major repair. Can we discuss this?"

Manager, "Sure."

Learn

Mr. Brown, "Please tell me your policy on calling customers before major repairs are made to their cars. Just list the three major issues for now."

Manager, "Our policy only has one issue. We call when the repair is over $300 or the customer sets a figure for repair. Your repair was $275 and the service advisor said you didn't set a limit for a call. You signed the repair form authorizing the repairs."

Mr. Brown, "So your policy is:

1. Major repairs = $300 or over
2. Call Customer = customer sets a figure for repair and repair exceeds the figure
3. Everyone signs a repair authorization form.

Is that correct?"

Manager, "Yes, you got it."

Mr. Brown, "I need to add that my request was for a call regardless of the cost of the repair, and I was not told I had to set a figure to be called."

Chapter Ten

Manager, "Mr. Brown, I see from your authorization form you did request a call, and our service representatives are trained to ask for a dollar amount."

Mr. Brown, "I need to add that I was not told I needed to state a dollar amount. I just signed the authorization form."

Understand

Mr. Brown, "Mr. Manager, it appears that the major differences center around 1) whether I should have been called and 2) what constitutes a 'major repair.' I signed the authorization form and the service representative put down on the form to call me before any major repairs were done. Can we talk about these two differences?"

Manager, "Well, I guess so, however, we have our policy which I have already stated."

Mr. Brown, "Yes, I did hear what your policy was for customers. May I ask, Is that policy written on the authorization form?"

Manager, "No, the service reps are trained to tell the customer at the time of service."

Mr. Brown, "Mr. Manager, knowing I said I was not informed of the policy, and knowing I had no way of reading it, does that make a difference in regards to a resolution of this matter?"

Manager, "The fact that we don't have it written on our forms matters more to me. Our service reps are very well trained."

Mr. Brown, "I hear you say that your service reps are well trained and not having the policy on the authorization form matters to you more in resolution of this matter. Can we resolve this now recognizing I had no knowledge of a dollar amount for major repairs?"

Manager, "O. K. , I see your point."

Empower

Mr. Brown, "Will you work with me on the repair bill? Can we discuss options"

Manager, "We have to pay for our parts, but we can work with the labor costs."

Mr. Brown, "So, if I pay for the parts, you will not charge me for labor?"

Manager, "That's right, labor on the brake job."

Mr. Brown, "Knowing this, I feel that is fair. Thank you."

In Consumer affairs, sometimes the Validation and Add blocks are all that is needed to stop a dispute from advancing into a real conflict. With proper validation and learning new information consumers are satisfied and de-escalate a dispute. I had a medical doctor tell me about an incident that proves this point. Her patient and his family were very angry with her because they had been urgently called for an office visit due to an alarming radiology report. In the meantime, before the planned office visit, the patient's radiology readings/results were discovered by the doctor to be inaccurate. Upon being

Chapter Ten

told the truth, the family began yelling at the doctor. The doctor remained calm and Validated their emotions instead of becoming defensive. She said,

"I see that you are very upset with me."

"I hear that this misreading by the radiologist has caused you grief and pain for several days."

"You thought your mother didn't have long to live."

"I need to validate your feelings, and add that the medical profession is not perfect."

"I regret that fact."

"I also need to add that as your doctor I have learned to check all medical tests I receive back from any source."

"This is for your protection."

"I have the accurate report here."

"May I tell you about the report?"

The act of Validating feelings and adding new information can stop a conflict from escalating. The family calmed down, apologized for their behavior, and then were ready to receive the accurate information.

The V.A.L.U.E. System in Family Disputes

In a comical example, students in one of my mediation classes were asked to Validate individuals for one week and report the results back to class. One student reported that his wife thought he was having an affair instead of attending the weekend mediation class. He was absolutely shocked and amazed. He naturally asked his wife what made her think that way. She responded that he was listening to her so intently and paying so much attention to her that he was not his normal self. She reasoned the attention must be due to his guilty feelings about an affair. The student laughed, and explained to his wife that he was just now learning to Validate others and it must be working! The class also had a good laugh. Other students also reported positive results, however, their results were not as exciting and captivating as his.

In other family disputes it is equally important to use as much of the V.A.L.U.E. System as necessary to prevent escalation of conflict and reach a resolution. In my family, for example, if I slip and forget to Validate ... I get in big trouble. Coming home one evening, I walked into the kitchen to greet my wife.

She said, "Boy, have I had a rough day at work."

Unfortunately my non–validating reply was, "Yea, I had a rough day too. Nothing seemed to work out right."

Chapter Ten

Immediately she responded, "You didn't validate me!"

I apologized and Validated her bad day. Then I asked her to tell me the major points of the day which I also Validated. She in turn Validated and heard about my rough day. After that we were both happy and had a pleasant evening forgetting our troubles at work.

Other family matters might not be so simple to resolve and require more use of the V.A.L.U.E. System. In today's economy there are many families in which both the husband and wife work. Disputes can arise over household chores, discipline of the children, helping the children with homework assignments, and car pool arrangements ... to name only a few. The V.A.L.U.E. System will apply to all of the above, and also to a dispute over work hours.

Tom and Beth both work full time outside their home. Tom is a sales representative for a manufacturing firm, and Beth is a legal secretary. They have two children, Todd and Sue, both involved in after school activities. Todd plays sports and Sue is on the drill team.

Tom and Beth have a conflict over both their work hours. Tom's hours are erratic and Beth usually has to stay late at the law office. The dispute has gone from the fermentation stage to the confrontation stage.

Validation

Tom, "I hear that you have to stay late at the office most days."

Beth, "Yes, I do. My work is very demanding with court deadlines."

Tom, "I also know that there are deadlines your boss needs to meet. Sometimes you don't get home until 8:00 p.m."

Beth, "Thank you, you're right. I appreciate your knowing this. I work hard."

Tom, "Beth, I know you work hard, and I appreciate it."

Add

Tom, "What I need to ADD to the discussion is that I have problems when I have to take a client for dinner. Dinner takes me until 9:00 p.m. or 10:00 p.m. at night. I can't take the kids to practice, and their coaches are saying they miss too many practices."

Beth, "Your schedule is much more flexible than mine. Why can't you change your schedule to meet the kids' schedule?"

Tom, "I hear you saying I need to change my schedule, correct?"

Beth, "Yes, I almost always have to work late. Always last minute stuff."

Tom, "Yes. It always seems that the law firm has last minute work to be done."

Learn

Tom, "Beth, can we talk about our schedules. Please give me the two or three things that absolutely control your schedule."

Beth, "The first thing is the day of the week. Next is my boss's case load. The third is the number of appointments my boss has during the day."

Tom, "Wow, there a lot of variables to your schedule."

Beth, "Yes, someday I need to get a 9–5 job."

Tom, "My schedule usually wraps around what clients I need to call on and which ones are coming in to the home office on business. I usually have to take them to dinner when they are in town."

Beth, "At least you can somewhat control your schedule."

Understand

Tom, "Let's look at the variables in our schedules and compare them. Maybe we can come up with something we haven't thought about. Something new."

Beth, "O. K., how do you want to do that?"

Tom, "Let's just brainstorm for a while."

Beth, "O. K." You go first."

Tom, "Your schedule is mainly controlled by your boss and his workload. So:

Beth's schedule = Boss's Workload.

My schedule is mostly controlled by my organization and out-of-town clients. So my schedule looks like this:

Tom's schedule = self organized + out-of-town clients."

Beth, "Yes, both are correct."

Tom, "The difference between our schedules is control of our time. You can't control any of your time in your present job, and I can't control when an out-of-town client wants to go to dinner."

Beth, "Yes, we both have control issues. HA! HA!"

Tom, "No, I'm serious. What we do at our jobs is the difference. We need to re-structure our jobs."

Beth, "Tom, get serious. A paralegal is a paralegal. We work overtime."

Tom, "I hear that, and agree."

Beth, "Tom, what option do we have? I am not going to quit my job and neither are you. We both need to work."

Tom, "Since the difference in our schedule is how we are controlled by others, let's think of an option to take back more control of our schedules without being fired."

Beth, "Fine, Tom, you start because I can't think of a single one."

Tom, "I could see if a junior sales representative could take clients out to dinner. I would have to clear that with my boss. That would put me more in control of some evenings."

Beth, "Knowing that, I could ask my boss if on the afternoons the kids had practice, if I could leave for an hour to take them to practice and come back to work. Could you could pick them up from practice."

Empower

Tom, "That sounds great. You take them and I can pick them up. That way I can work a full day."

Beth, "I still have to clear this with my boss."

Tom, "I do too, but at least we have a plan for now. Let's finalize this tomorrow after we talk to our bosses."

Beth, "O. K. That was easy enough."

The V.A.L.U.E. System at Work

Co-worker disputes can cause friction, and therefore need to be resolved as soon as possible. I have mediated employment disputes over company policies, discrimination disputes of all types, religion in the workplace, and other similar disputes that arise between employees working eight hours a day together. An interesting dispute can arise with loans between co-workers. The money is loaned and not paid back, yet the co-worker asks for another loan. A dispute arises between the two co-workers. Let's use the V.A.L.U.E. System again in this dispute and see how it plays out. Let's call the co-worker who loaned the money, Chase, and the co-worker who borrowed the money is Martha.

Validation

Chase, "I hear, Martha, that you need another small loan to get you through this pay period. Is that right?"

Martha, "That's right. I'm sorry I have not been able to pay you back for the first loan, but things have been really rough for me financially."

Chase, "I hear you saying that things have been really rough for you lately and you are sorry you can't pay me for the first loan."

Martha, "Oh yes! I am so glad you understand. Can I have the new loan. It's only $500.00 for a week or so.

Chase, "Is it right that you want $500.00 for only a week or so?"

Martha, "Yes, Please I really need the money."

Add

Chase, "Martha, I hear what you need, and I would like to add that I need to be paid back for the first loan before I think of loaning you any more money. Can we talk about this?"

Martha, "Oh yes, because I really need the money."

Learn

Chase, "Martha, please tell me two or three reasons I should loan you more money."

Martha, "First, Chase, my rent is due on my apartment and I had to take my baby to the emergency room and pay a deductible. You know I am a single mom and my former husband has not been paying child support payments."

Chase, "Well, Martha, I can validate those are three solid reasons for needing a loan. Let me tell you my thinking please. First, I already loaned you $300.00 last month for an emergency. Second, I was not paid back like you promised, and third, how do I know you will pay me the $800.00?"

Martha, "Chase, I promise you I will pay you back. I will even pay you interest on the money."

Understand

Chase, "Martha, I believe you need the money and will pay me interest on the $800.00. What is the difference between last time I loaned you money and this time? I need to know how you can pay me $800.00 plus interest this next month when you couldn't pay me $300.00 this month."

Martha, "Oh, I can explain the difference. I am working overtime on the new project, and that should give me the $300.00 I owe you from the first loan. Then the attorney general's office has collected some back child support that will allow me to give you $500.00 plus reasonable interest on the total $800.00. The only problem is I won't get any of the money until the end of the month."

Chase, "Will you sign something in writing that you owe me $800.00 plus interest at 5% annually until the money is paid at the end of the month?"

Martha, "Yes, of course I will if that is what you need."

Chase, "What happens if you don't pay me in the full by the end of the month?"

Martha, "Chase, I will, but just in case I will pay you $300.00 and then $100.00 a week until the note is paid. That's if my child support is delayed."

Chase, "Well, knowing that, I might be able to loan you the extra money. Can I see the child support letters

Chapter Ten

from the attorney general's office about the time you will get your money?"

Martha, "Sure, but please don't spread this confidential information around the office."

Chase, "If I trust you enough to make the loans, you will have to trust me also."

Martha, "Sure, Chase, I'm sorry. I'm just a bit sensitive now about my situation, thanks!"

Empower

Chase, "O. K. , Martha, I will loan you the extra money knowing your situation. But, I need something in writing."

Martha, "Anything you say. I just really need the money now."

Both Chase and Martha can draw up a written empowerment plan. The plan would include the exact date Martha was to pay back the money, the exact amount of interest on the money, and how she was to pay the money – check or cash. Also the plan would include a provision for the partial payments as discussed in the Understand phase. Of course, Chase would not lend her the new money until he saw the letter on child support payments from the attorney general's office.

If Chase had not been so agreeable or if Martha's reasons had not appealed to Chase's sense of helping others, the dispute may have taken a different turn. Chase would probably have VALIDATED Martha's needs, then ADDED several reasons for not being able to loan her the additional $500.00. He may have told her he had extra bills himself, had a trip he was saving for, or simply he didn't feel comfortable making the second loan. Upon discussion, Martha would have stated her same reasons. If these reasons didn't make a difference to Chase, he would probably ask for a resolution based upon his reasons. Because Martha was sure to receive $300.00 by working overtime, they could set a time for the re-payment of that money. She might even pay him interest on the $300.00 from the date of the loan and the principle amount when she got her pay check. They could put this resolution in writing, if needed. Chase might suggest a pay-day loan for the $500.00. The availability of a commercial pay-day loan may be new information to Martha. Such new information might resolve her new loan issues. Chase however, will have to decide if he wants to be the office banker in the future.

Of course the various resolutions depend upon how the parties perceive their needs at the time of the dispute. The important aspect is to use the V.A.L.U.E. System to engage and manage the conflict is a respectful manner ... especially between people who work together day-in-and-day-out. Resolving the conflict early prevents escalation that could ruin a good working environment or relationship.

Chapter Ten

The V.A.L.U.E. System in Landlord/Tenant Disputes

Conflict between a tenant and a landlord can be troubling, especially if there is local management and a head office in another location. Furthermore, if local management changes hands while a tenant is still on a lease there can be disputes based upon the different styles of management. Using the V.A.L.U.E. System is extremely important if one is a tenant, as apartment lease contracts usually favor the apartment owners ... although tenants do have valuable rights in most states.

In these disputes, the dynamic usually finds the tenant upset about a repair not completed, a contract clause, or a policy interpretation. The apartment manager is often on the defensive. Using the V.A.L.U.E. System can help improve the dynamics ... especially Validation. Let's take an example of a new manager administering a policy for use of the community room in an apartment complex.

Validation

Tenant, "Mr. Manager, I received this written notice that the community room was only for use by residents. No outside groups can use the community room for their meetings. Did I get that right?"

Mr. Manager, "Yes, you got that completely correct. We have a policy that states just that. It is in your lease."

Tenant, "Oh, that policy is a part of our lease?"

Mr. Manager, "Yes, would you like to see it?"

Add

Tenant, "Oh, I believe you. I would like to ADD that the previous manager allowed our organization to use the community room because we had three tenants who were members. I also would like to add that each tenant invited two people as their guest. We only had nine people at any one time."

Learn

Mr. Manager, "The policy clearly states that only residents and invited guests can use the community room. No outside organizations may reserve the room."

Tenant, "So, what I hear you say is that we can only have guests in the community room. Is that correct?"

Mr. Manager, "That is correct, but it cannot be used for an organization meeting. That is the policy."

Understand

Tenant, "I need to know the difference between having an organization meeting in the community room and having a guest in the community room."

Mr. Manager, "The difference is you are having a business meeting in a community space. Other tenants

Chapter Ten

may want to use the space for themselves, however, they can't because there are too many outside people talking and having meetings in the community room. We have had complaints."

Tenant, "Please tell me the difference in reserving the community room, as a tenant, for a function, which is allowed, and our situation."

Mr. Manager, "When a tenant reserves the room for his function it is usually on the weekend and the other tenants can see by the sign up sheet the community room is reserved in advance."

Tenant, "So, the real difference is 1) a reservation in advance, and 2) a weekend function. Is that right?"

Mr. Manager, "Well, I guess if you put it that way, you're right."

Tenant, "In that case, can we talk about this difference?"

Mr. Manager, "Well, I guess we could. But a policy is a policy."

Tenant. "I need to Validate that a policy is a policy. I would like to ADD that the only difference appears to be when we use the community room and making a reservation for its use. If any of our three member tenants makes a reservation on the weekday, can we use the room for our guests and call it a function? We would serve coffee and cake and talk."

Mr. Manager, "No, it's not a function, it is an organizational meeting. There is a difference."

Tenant, "Please tell me what difference it makes to the other tenants if they still can't use the room because it is reserved for a party or a function."

Mr. Manager, "On that account, I see no difference. The policy does not define a party or function, only that a community room is for tenants and their guests."

Tenant, "There also appears to be a difference if we used the community room during the week. Is that right?"

Mr. Manager, "Yes, the complaints were that the tenants could not use the room to play cards or have parties during the weekends."

Empower

Tenant, "So, if we reserved the community room for a Monday night when usage is low, and had our members as guests would that be O. K.?"

Mr. Manager, "Well, any tenant can reserve the room for a function and it is hardly used on Monday nights. Just have your formal business organizational meeting before or after your function."

Tenant, "I don't want to lie about our organization and it's use of the community room."

Mr. Manager, "If you will have your meetings on Monday nights and reserve the room, then I will allow you to use it. However, you must reserve the room one week in advance. There will be no reservations weeks in advance. Other tenants may want a Monday

Chapter Ten

night reservation also. Furthermore, if I get any valid complaints the deal is off. Alright?"

Tenant, "If there are complaints, can we talk about them together?"

Mr. Manager, "You bet we will talk."

Tenant, "O. K. We can abide by your rules on this policy. Thanks."

Sometimes in a dispute there is a difference without a valid distinction ... as in the case just illustrated. However, one must work through the V.A.L.U.E. process for the party in power to see that there is no valid distinction. As seen in Diagram XIII and discussed in Chapter 6, education of the party in power is essential for conflict resolution.

Each of the forgoing illustrations contained only one major issue in the conflict or dispute. However, if there is more than one issue in controversy, follow the steps in the V.A.L.U.E. System for each issues. Keeping issues separated is a good idea in conflict resolution. That way each issue can stand on its own for a full discussion. If the issues do overlap, try combining them into one issue or a new concept. Then follow the V.A.L.U.E. System on the combined or new concept.

Keep in mind you may tend to forget to Validate the new concepts or combined issues. Jumping into the ADD or LEARN phases at that point may be premature. You can quickly Validate that the combined or new concept is on the table as such, and Add your perspective. Then start the LEARN phase and you will be on track.

Seeing Through The Wall

    Once you learn the key phrases and adapt them to your style it will be easy for you to move from one phase to the next quickly. Also you will be able to move from one issue to another with ease. If one issue hinges on another, set a priority for which issues will be discussed first. The result of that issue may change the Learn phase discussion of the next issue.

    You can be as flexible as you desire with the order of issues as long as you keep the discussion in the order of the V.A.L.U.E. System.

KEY POINTS

Chapter 1

1. Although today the outright manifestations of conflict are spotlighted by terrorism, hate crimes and violent acts of aggression, we all must realize that our government or other institutions are not adept enough to resolve these problems. Each of us must learn to engage and manage conflict in order to solve our own problems which will, in turn, cause a collective shift in the problem re–solving capacity of our culture. No longer can we hide from this personal responsibility. Each of us has to learn how to manage and resolve conflict in our own personal world of accountability.

2. As Einstein implies, we must re–look at issues in a new way. In other words, we must learn a process to "re–solve" our personal conflict. We need to adopt a new personal process to properly engage and resolve conflict right from the start. An effective resolution process incorporates interpersonal action and thought. *We can look at conflict differently. We can discover a process to foster resolution of conflict.*

Chapter 2

1. Conflict is an *ongoing* state of disagreement or disharmony that has the potential to ultimately advance from fermentation to a state of open, prolonged fighting or war.

2. *What often looks like no conflict is really circumstances fermenting or breaking down.* Think of developing conflict as the process of making a delicious fruit topping from scratch. My mother makes a delicious dessert topping by using a starter solution to break down and dissolve fresh fruit. But the process takes time to chemically work. Although I open the covered bowl and sense nothing happening, the starter solution is fermenting and chemically breaking down the fruit. What appears on the surface as nothing happening is not reality. The dessert process is called fermentation or a process of breaking things down. Conflict works the same way in its first stage.

3. Resolving a conflict based upon old information is very difficult, as there is nothing new to work with toward resolution.

Chapter 3

1. The V.A.L.U.E. System posits that validating others and their perspectives, discovering and discussing differences, not commonalities, resolves conflict. The V.A.L.U.E. System is based upon a process to uncover and learn others' differences, then explore and understand these

differences in order to expose new information. Once this new information is discovered, people have new reason to resolve their problems with others. Both parties may not like what they see, hear or feel; however, they can live with the resolution because they know and finally understand each other's perspective.

Chapter 4

1. Individuals who are not allowed to "be" in conflict will fight for the right to have their conflict, which ultimately means to have the right to their own perspectives. Thus, one can appreciate that allowing an individual the right to "be" in conflict is one of the very first steps to resolving any conflict.

2. Validating statements are verbal and accurate repetitions of:
   + What a person stated
   + The feelings attached to the statements
   + A reflection of the environment surrounding the statement
   + A request for accuracy

   Validating statements are made with a non–patronizing and neutral tone of voice.

3. Validation needs to take place as early as possible in the process to prevent the other person from having to press his position over and over again until he feels you have heard him.

4. Remember – validation is not agreement. Validation is a process, not an end result. Validation of the person, her ideas and concepts helps to move the discussion process on because it lowers the defensiveness of both parties. When we validate we do not agree fully; however, we give immediate recognition to the other person's perspective on a conflict issue.

5. Validation changes the dynamics of the dispute process and opens up communication. Although validation is the first block in the V.A.L.U.E. System, it needs to be used throughout the dispute process when there is a need to acknowledge a new idea, position, concept, feeling or person surfaces.

Chapter 5

1. By using the "add" technique, each person can feel validated in what he is attempting to express. At a minimum, each person is heard and not discounted by the other individual. This addition of information can be viewed by the other party as new information and not as a discount of his perception. This concept is important to the building blocks of conflict resolution.

2. The use of "I" based statements allows you to own your idea and not blame the other person. Also, the use of a "need" based statement allows the other person to see how important your perception or belief is to you. In combination, an "I" and "need" based statement express ownership rights in a belief without blaming the other person.

CHAPTER 6

1. Learning is a full exploration of the substance of each person's issues involved in a conflict. This newly learned information shows the person's meaning behind his issues and can be conceptualized in a few words.

2. Reforming and Recycling
   The goal of the Learn block is to discover the substantive meaning of each party's issues and recycle or transform that meaning into a new concept. This transformation is done by:

   a. Asking each party to define in three parts what his issue means to him.

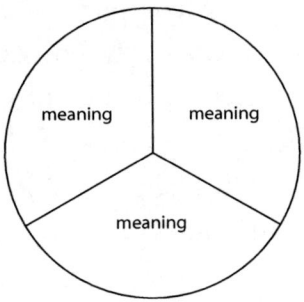

   (diagram: a circle divided into three sections, each labeled "meaning")

   b. If possible, combine meanings to determine one or more central themes and name that theme in no more than (7) seven words as a new concept.

   c. Get each party's agreement of this new concept or phrase, and validate the concept.

   d. Set up an agenda for discussion of these conceptual differences in the Understand block.

Chapter 7

1. In the concept of the V.A.L.U.E. System, differences mean perceptions that are opposite. *Distinctions are different characteristics of the same concept ... the subparts.*

Chapter 8

1. A solution and a resolution differ within the context of the V.A.L.U.E. System. A solution is the answer or final disposition of a problem. Many times, only looking for a final disposition, implies a negotiation tug–of–war where each side pulls as hard as she can to get what she needs based upon her original position. A resolution looks at the underlying explanation for the problem and works with the substantive issues that form the conflict. The focus of the resolution deals with joint discussion and problem solving, not on negotiation techniques to achieve a final disposition or solution. Solution implies negotiation, and resolution implies joint in depth problem solving.

LIST OF DIAGRAMS

Diagram I – Building Blocks of the V.A.L.U.E. System 52
Diagram II – An Employee's Perspective of
  "Employment Fairness" 56
Diagram III – Just Compensation 58
Diagram IV – Win / Win Options................................. 59
Diagram V – Components of Communication 61
Diagram VI – A Synopsis of the V.A.L.U.E. System 64
Diagram VII – Validation Touches Many Aspects
  of a Person 66
Diagram VIII – Organization of Perspective / Position 93
Diagram IX – Beliefs Supporting Position of
  "I want a divorce".. 96
Diagram X – Different Beliefs in a Divorce Conflict 97
Diagram XI – Power & Knowledge Paradigm 107
Diagram XII – Power & Knowledge Imbalance Conflict 108
Diagram XIII – Resolving Power & Knowledge
  Imbalance Conflict 109
Diagram XIV – Transforming Information 113
Diagram XV – Different Beliefs in Divorce Conflict............ 114

Diagram XVI – "No Trust" Issue 115
Diagram XVII – Drilling for New Meaning 116
Diagram XVIII – "Love" Issue 117
Diagram XIX – Husband's Reasons 120
Diagram XX – Wife's Reasons 121
Diagram XXI – Wife's Issues Recycled 122
Diagram XXII – Transformed Issues 123
Diagram XXIII – Categorization of Transformed Issues 125
Diagram XXIV – Paring of Values, Beliefs and Attitudes 127
Diagram XXV – Husband's Dialog 136
Diagram XXVI – Wife's Dialog 136
Diagram XXVII – Budget Sub Points 147
Diagram XXVIII – A Typical Negotiation "Tug of War" 155
Diagram XXIX– Empowered Resolution 156
Diagram XXX – A New Way to Achieve 100% 157
Diagram XXXI – The V.A.L.U.E. System 166

ABOUT THE AUTHOR

Dr. James W. Gibson

Dr. James Gibson is an attorney, mediator, and educator with an extensive background in alternative dispute resolution and conflict management. James is a frequent speaker on conflict management at state, regional and national conferences. He was awarded the highest honor obtainable by a mediator in the State of Texas by the Texas Association of Mediators in 2007. Dr. Gibson received this award based upon eighteen years of contributions to the advancement of mediation in Texas and the nation. Dr. Gibson also served on the Board of the Texas Mediators Credentialing Association as Secretary, and was honored in 2009 by the Texas Mediators Credentialing Association with an endowed scholarship in his name. He was formerly on the Board of Directors of the Texas Association of

Mediators, the Texas Mediators Trainers Roundtable, and is past President and Treasurer of the Greater Houston Chapter Society of Professionals in Dispute Resolution (now ACR). A member of the State Bar of Texas, he has been honored for outstanding service to that organization's Alternative Dispute Resolution Section.

He is co-author of *Capitalizing on Conflict*, published by Davies-Black, Palo Alto, California, April, 2002. After release, Harvard Business School placed *Capitalizing on Conflict* on their Book Recommendation Library List, and it also won an award as one of the best business books in 2002.

He has written or contributed to various training manuals, and published the first training manual for criminal mediation in Texas. Other publications have been featured in **Texas Trial Lawyer, Alternative Resolutions, Texas Mediator**, the newsletter of the Texas Court of Criminal Appeals, publications of The State Bar of Texas, and Texas Young Lawyers Association.

Since 1996, he has trained mediators through Southern Methodist University Certificate and Masters Program in Dispute Resolution, Sam Houston State University, Texas A&M University, Texas Woman's University, The University of Houston-Clear Lake, Our Lady of the Lake, and The Citadel by conducting seminars in Basic Mediation, Advanced Mediation, Family Mediation, Mediation of Employer/Employee Disputes, Ethics, Criminal Justice, and Advanced Communication Skills. In addition to his mediation training, James serves as Students' Legal Advisor at Sam Houston State University. He also mediates disputes for private clients, and consults with public and private organizations on the development and implementation of alternative dispute resolution systems. He specializes in highly complex interpersonal cases in both political and non−political settings.

Dr. Gibson received his B.B.A. degree from the University of Texas at Austin, a Master of Science from Sam Houston State University, and his Juris Doctor from Southern Methodist University School of Law.

ORDER FORM

Seeing Through The Wall

Four ways to order copies of **_Seeing Through The Wall_**:

1) Online at http://www.HighPointPublishing.com
2) Call HighPoint Publishing, Inc at 1–512–858–2727
3) Copy this order form, fill it in and fax to 1–512–532–0783
4) Visit your local bookstore!

Item	Quantity	Price Each	Total Price
Seeing Through The Wall ISBN–13: 978–1–933190–20–4	(max 10)	$ 24.95	
Sales Tax *Texas residents only!*		$2.62 per book 8.25%	
Shipping and Handling		**$4.95** *for one book* **$9.95** *for 2–10 books*	
		Total Cost *prices subject to change without notice*	

Name: _____

Address: _____

City: _____ State: _____ Zip Code: _____

Telephone: _____

Credit Card Number: _____ CVV: _____

Expiration date: _____ Email: _____

Orders placed by fax must be shipped to the credit card billing address.
Checks, Money Orders or bulk orders of more than ten books, please call.

HighPoint Publishing, Inc
3975 US Highway 290 East
Dripping Springs, TX 78620
(512) 858–2727